BUREAUCRACY AND DEVELOPMENT
IN
THE ARAB WORLD

INTERNATIONAL STUDIES
IN
SOCIOLOGY AND SOCIAL ANTHROPOLOGY

General Editor

K. ISHWARAN

VOLUME LI

JOSEPH G. JABBRA

BUREAUCRACY AND DEVELOPMENT
IN
THE ARAB WORLD

BUREAUCRACY AND DEVELOPMENT IN THE ARAB WORLD

EDITED BY

JOSEPH G. JABBRA

Saint Mary's University

E.J. BRILL

LEIDEN · NEW YORK · KØBENHAVN · KÖLN

1989

Library of Congress Cataloging-in-Publication Data

Bureaucracy and development in the Arab world / edited by
  Joseph G. Jabbra.
    p.   cm. — (International studies in sociology and social
  anthropology, ISSN 0074-8684; v. 51)
    ISBN 9004091947
    1. Arab countries—Politics and government—1945-
  2. Bureaucracy-Arab countries. 3. Arab countries—
  Economic development—Political aspects. I. Jabbra,
  Joseph G. II. Series.
  JQ1850.A5B87   1989
  338.9'00917'4927—dc20   89-17346
                                                               CIP

                    ISSN   0074-8684
                    ISBN   90 04 09194 7

PRINTED IN THE NETHERLANDS BY E. J. BRILL

CONTENTS

Bureaucracy and Development in the Arab World

JOSEPH G. JABBRA

Saint Mary's University, Halifax, Canada

Introduction

IN THE WAKE OF WORLD WAR II, Arab leaders were euphoric at winning independence for their countries from colonial powers. However, their euphoria was dampened by the challenge of nation-building. Although Arab leaders were concerned primarily about staying in power, they also spent significant amounts of time, energy, and money to promote socio-economic and political development in their countries. They expanded educational opportunities for their citizens (Abu-Laban and Abu-Laban 1986:1), they attempted to develop industry, commerce, and urban growth (Stephens 1976); and in a number of cases, they struggled to foster the services sector in their economies. In the oil-producing countries of the Arab world, the political leadership continues to consider comprehensive development as its major challenge and diversification of the economy as one of its major goals (Kubursi 1984).

In their efforts to move their countries forward, Arab leaders fully realized the extent to which bureaucracy was central to their development endeavors. Thus Arab leaders declared the 1980s as "the decade of Arab administrative development" (Zoubi 1982:7). Bureaucracies in the Arab world, as in all societies, were called upon to maintain law and order, execute decisions of the political leadership, and carry out the day-to-day functions of the state (Al Nimir and Palmer 1982:93); as well, they were called upon to be involved in socio-economic and political development. In the 1950s and 1960s, the bureaucracy in the Arab world represented, to many leaders an orderly alternative to social and cultural revolutionary chaos; its potential role in development was acknowledged and political leaders were admonished to involve it in national comprehensive planning, in a rapidly growing system of primary and secondary education, in extensive industrialization programs, and in urban growth and construction (Ayubi 1986:89). In most instances, there were no other agencies capable of carrying out the responsibilities of development and of responding adequately to citizens' new demands. The private sector was mainly concerned with profit making in a politically stable environment. Most Arab countries did not provide political stability and security and therefore the private sector preferred investing in Western countries where political stability prevailed and profits were secure (Al Nimir and Palmer 1982:93).

Thus, a common belief prevailed in the Arab world that if the bureaucracy could not manage to provide an adequate level of services, the political leadership would find it difficult to cope with the increasing demands of citizens; it was also commonly held that, should the bureaucracy not be able to play an effective role in development, political and socio-economic problems of staggering magnitudes were likely to ensue and threaten to dislocate the very fabric of society (Al-Hegelan and Palmer 1985:48).

Unfortunately, Arab countries were to find soon that the bureaucracy was ill-equipped to carry out the daunting task of development; its membership and even in some cases its top echelons did not have the necessary educational level, training and skills to enable them to carry out their responsibilities with competence, efficiency, and effectiveness. In order to respond to this shortcoming, Arab leaders felt that administrative development must accompany if not precede development administration. Accordingly, they proceeded to adopt wholesale Western technology and methods to modernize their bureaucracies. They invited experts from the United States, Europe, Japan, the Soviet Union, China, and other Eastern block countries to give them advice on how best to achieve administrative development. Furthermore, students and public servants were sent abroad on handsome scholarships to train in the best schools. They were expected to return home, use their newly-acquired skills, and implement the best and latest technology to improve the calibre and quality of the public service in their own countries (Ayubi 1986:89).

By the 1970s, Arab leaders began to realize that neither had their efforts to develop the administrative quality and capacity of their bureaucracy been successful, nor had their aspirations to achieve political and socio-economic development been satisfied. The bureaucracy was unable to reform itself and consequently could not improve its service to the public. In fact, "the bureaucracy has become an instrument of domination and the bureaucrats have turned into a new exploitative class" (Ayubi 1986: 97).

On the whole, Arab bureaucracies have not been able to contribute significantly to finding solutions to problems of development and thus the standards of living and the amenities of life are still low for the majority of Arab citizens. Poverty still persists with the basic needs for water, food, shelter, education, and health still far from satisfied. The adoption of Western technology and the repeated attempts at industrialization have failed to create enough jobs for an ever-growing labour force.

Reasons and Proposed Solutions for the Failure of Arab bureaucracies in Development

What are the reasons for this poor record of development administration in the Arab world? El-Fathali and Chackerian (1983) and Palmer and Nakib (1978) have provided a series of reasons which may explain the failure of Arab bureaucracies to meet the challenges of development. Remedies have been proposed by Ayubi (1986) who emphasized the contingency approach, counselling Arab leaders to learn from the successes of their bureaucracies and expand on them, and by Jabbra and Jabbra (1983) who believe that Ayubi's approach, while necessary, is not sufficient by itself; they propose a new process of socialization in Arab society as well as in Arab bureaucracies. Let us, however, first summarize the reasons for the failure of Arab bureaucracies in promoting development.

1. *Newness and Limitations of Arab Bureaucratic Structure*

Most bureaucratic structures in the Arab world date back to the post World War II era. They were established with the help of colonial powers and inherited colonial administrative values and goals after independence. As the role of Arab governments began to expand, existing administrative structures were strained and could not respond adequately to the significant changes taking place in Arab society.

2. *Traditional Arab Culture*

The behavior of Arab public servants is still much influenced by certain aspects of traditional Arab culture, such as the primacy of the family. Thus, they tend to be particularistic and to put the needs of their families or denominations before those of the state (Nakib and Palmer 1976:15).

3. *Concentration and Diffusion of Authority*

Concentration of authority is a typical feature of Arab bureaucracies. Both formal and informal authority is concentrated at the top of the administrative hierarchy. Below the top, however, one finds that authority and responsibility are diffuse. This situation has led to a series of problems, including "red tape", poor coordination, lack of adequate communication, vagueness in job description and overlapping duties, functions and jurisdictions (Ayubi 1977).

4. *Lack of Reliable Data Bases*

Bureaucracies in the Arab world have not yet succeeded in developing reliable data bases useful for the formulation of development policies and the introduction of needed reforms. According to El-Fathali and Chackerian (1983: 196), it is clear that without reliable data, plans for administrative reforms and for economic and social development will not reflect the real needs, priorities and resources of Arab society.

5. *Political Interference*

Whatever the particular form of government in the Arab world, the political leadership is likely to interfere with the bureaucracy in order to protect itself and promote its interests. If a charismatic leader in the Arab world is prevented by the buraucracy from acting freely, he either ignores it or bypasses it and claims before the public that it is not carrying out its responsibilities properly (El-Fathali and Palmer 1980: Micaud 1969). Such interference is bound to cause confusion in the bureaucracy and distract it form pursuing development priorities and responding to the real needs of the citizens.

6. *Mismatches in Training and Education*

Another serious problem facing Arab bureaucracies is the lack of qualified people, poor training, and incongruency between the needs of the state and available educational and training facilities and programs. Several factors can account for this situation. First, among Arab students who receive their education and training abroad, a significant number do not return home, thus depriving their countries of their talents and skills. Moreover, of those who do return, a large number seek employment in the private sector or with multinational corporations where they are lured by high salaries, significant material incentives, and much better working conditions. Second, a large number of educated people who join the public service are often given jobs which do not match their level of education and training (Ayubi 1977; Iskandar 1964: Shuster 1969). And finally, the program emphases of educational and training institutions are unrelated to the needs of the state. For a long period of time and for cultural and cost reasons, the Arab world has neglected technical fields of study. This situation has resulted in a shortage of qualified technical people and a surplus of people in the social sciences and the humanities.

7. *Poor Relations between Bureaucracy and Citizens*

The relationship between the bureaucracy and citizens has been poor in Arab countries. Arab citizens do not participate positively and actively in the development of their countries. Thus, they receive public services as a matter of favor rather than of right. According to El-Fathali (1975), without the responsible participation of the public in the development of society, it is difficult to envisage how the Arab world can progress in response to citizens' needs and demands.

8. *Corruption*

Corruption is a persistent feature of bureaucracy nearly everywhere in the Arab world. Many reasons explain the prevalence of corruption in the Arab world. These include public servants' weak commitment to the state, the distance between them and the masses, their lack of appreciation of the concept of public service, inadequate salaries and fringe benefits, and the absence or weakness of key institutions (Waterbury 1973, 1976; Kisirwani 1971). According to El-Fathali and Chackerian (1983:197), corruption has become so widespread in the Arab world that many public servants look at it as an acceptable and legitimate route to success. Those who succeed become very respectable in their communities and models to be followed by others. Unfortunately, the practices of corruption are being internalized by younger generations and will become part of their value systems if no measures to stop them are implemented. With corruption deeply rooted in the attitudes and behavior of public servants, development will cease to be their goal and self-enrichment will replace it as the focus of their attention.

9. *Staffing*

Bureaucracies in the Arab world can be divided into two groups. One group (Egypt, Morocco, and the Sudan) experiences overstaffing. This has resulted in confusing and poorly coordinated administrative structures. In this group of countries, public service employment has become a way to disguise unemployment and a means of absorbing young graduates into the job market. This disguised unemployment leads to a low degree of accountability, low productivity, and inefficiency on the part of public servants. The second group (Saudi Arabia, Kuwait, Libya, Qatar, and the United Arab Emirates) has understaffed bureaucracies, with many unqualified employees. These countries cope with the problem by hiring foreign personnel. This practice has caused severe problems, such as lack of continuity and consistency. Moreover, although foreign personnel fill vacancies in the public service, they are often not fully utilized. They also complain about not fully understanding their roles and responsibilities. Furthermore, the diversified background of foreign employees has contributed to poor internal and external communication.

The Contingency Approach

Some scholars have questioned the impact of cultural traits on development. In this context Professor Ayubi (1986:98) warns us against the risks of jumping to the quick conclusions that cultural and structural factors can explain the failures of Arab bureaucracies to promote and sustain socio-economic and political development. Ayubi maintains that Palmer and Nakib (1978) are not unique in asserting that some administrative problems in the Arab world find their roots in Arab culture. However, he questions their emphasis on the fact that many of the structural problems in Arab bureaucracies are "overt manifestations of deeper cultural, behavioral and political problems endemic to the area" (Palmer and Nakib 1978:20).

Ayubi contends that the cultural explanation of administrative problems is often lacking in explanatory power as well as in prescriptive value. For example, it fails to explain Japanese economic prowess. Japan has been successful in bringing about modernization and raising productivity while maintaining aspects of traditional Japanese culture which are considered by modernization theorists to be unfavorable to development. The cultural explanation is of little prescriptive value because even when it submits for our scrutiny factual evidence, it bases its expectations on the hope that the whole society will change its attitudes and patterns of behavior in order to create a more favorable environment for the proper functioning of the bureaucracy. It is obvious that while this hope is idealistic, it is tinged with a pessimistic and helpless note.

Ayubi counsels us to start from the last page of the report by Palmer and Nakib where the authors analyze the strengths as well as the weakness of Arab bureaucracies. Palmer and Nakib (1978:23) suggests that "a thorough survey of existing data would enable us to study in detail those facets of Arab public administration that have worked well, so that other Arab states might benefit from their experience." Ayubi admonishes Arab leadership to begin taking stock and learning from the successes and failures of their bureaucracies in their endeavours to cope with the challenge of development. Careful analysis of the various experiments in the Arab world, with their successes and failures, would be a good start. This should be supplemented by comparative studies of exceptional successes in similar contexts in other third world countries. According to Paul (1982:4-5), "the insights and understanding to be gained from high performers will be far more valuable than the incremental gains to be derived from further investigations of low performance about which we already know a great deal".

Ayubi (1986:102) also urges Arab leaders not to engage in the business of comparing an abstract Arab society to an abstract Western society. This exercise is futile. In Ayubi's judgement it would be better to analyze the Arab values and practices which are conducive to good bureaucratic performance and useful to development. These elements are likely to instill self-confidence in both Arab public servants and citizens.

The Socialization Approach

While Ayubi's approach is commendable, it cannot alone help us eliminate the bureaucratic obstacles to development in the Arab world. It must be accompanied by a new process of socialization covering Arab society as well as Arab bureaucracies (Jabbra and Jabbra 1983). This approach is premised upon the understanding that the causes for the poor record of development administration and administrative development in the Arab world are imbedded in the social settings of Arab bureaucracies. Thus the relationship that binds bureaucracies to their social settings makes it difficult to reform the former without the latter. Already in 1947, Robert Dahl pointed out that "we cannot afford to ignore the relationship between public administration and its social setting". Therefore in order to eradicate the bureaucratic obstacles to development in the Arab world, we must not only follow Ayubi's admonition but also find effective means to eliminate from both Arab bureaucracies and their social settings, the attitudes and patterns of behavior which continuously give them strengths. Jabbra and Jabbra (1983:140) suggest that a new process of socialization, strengthened by a well-publicized code of ethics and implemented within the Arab public services and among the public at large, appears to be, with Ayubi's approach, the best remedy for the bureaucractic obstacles to development.

Organization of the Issue

This publication was prepared with the hope of shedding light on the relationship between bureaucracy and development in the Arab world. It contains seven articles focussing on different aspects of that relationship.

First, Monte Palmer and his colleagues address the question of bureaucratic innovation in three Arab countries: the Sudan, Saudi Arabia, and Egypt. By innovation the authors mean the willingness of public servants to develop and implement new approaches to administrative and social problems. The authors contend that if public servants in these three countries cannot provide innovative solutions to their countries' problems, their role as agencies of socio-economic and political development will be limited. They also contend that innovation should not be limited to the higher echelons of the bureaucracy but should characterize the entire bureaucratic apparatus.

The data which form the empirical basis for their analysis of innovation are derived from parallel surveys of senior public officials in the Sudan and Saudi Arabia, and a general survey of the Egyptian bureaucracy. On the basis of their data, the authors conclude that the public servants of the three countries are not innovative and are not inclined to take risks. The authors conclude that this situation must be altered if Arab bureaucrats are to play a dynamic role in the development process.

While Palmer and his associates analyse the relationship between innovation and development in three Arab countries, Mukhtar Al-Assam begins his article on the Sudan by stating that the Sudanese bureaucracy played a major role in the country's political development. It achieved independence, established political parties and a parliamentary regime, and assumed the integrative function in Sudanese society. After independence, the Sudanese bureaucracy was considered the only national institution which could claim to represent all of Sudanese society. Moreover, while politicians were busy contending for power, the running of the country was left to the bureaucracy. Thus socio-economic planning and rural development have come to be considered as purely administrative activities.

However, despite the Sudanese bureaucracy's high level of education, its relatively high level of functional capability, and its relevance to socio-economic and political development, the author contends that it has failed as an agent of development. He argues that administrative inefficiency, obsolete administrative structures, lack of coordination, bureaucratic in-fighting and jealousies have led to poor implementation and execution of government policies and thus have constituted powerful obstacles to development.

In contrast to Al-Assam's negative conclusions regarding the role of the Sudanese bureaucracy in development, Ibrahim Al-Awaji paints a more positive picture of the role of Saudi local administration in development. With the oil boom in Saudi Arabia, new organizations were established to respond to the pressures of development in the areas of municipal works, electricity, water, communication, and road services. The Saudi national government established new regulations to raise the quality of local management to the levels of national management. The author points to several shortcomings of the local bureaucracy in carrying out socio-economic and political development policies: diversity in the number and level of local bureaucratic structures; low educational qualifications of local public officials; imbalance between the local agencies' executive authority and their responsibilities; and a serious degree of duplication and lack or coordination of services.

Despite these problems, the author contends that the Saudi local administrative system has been active in the dynamic development of the Kingdom. This active role has been promoted by the national economic development plans which have emphasized the development of the regions through the establishment of regional development centres. The responsibility this emphasis has brought has strengthened the ability of local administrative agencies to respond successfully to the challenges of development.

While Ibrahim Al-Awaji focussed on the role of the Saudi local administration in development, Nazih Ayubi argues that since the adoption of the open door policy in the mid-seventies, the Egyptian bureaucracy has continued to grow. Its growth in terms of personnel and expenditure, however, has been in the areas associated with the repressive functions of the state, rather than in areas related to the service or socio-economic functions of the Egyptian bureaucracy. Moreover, the Egyptian bureaucracy has experienced a change in its role from that of a developer to that of a producer or a trader.

It is important to note that until the declaration of the open door policy, the public sector in Egypt played a major role in economic development. The introduction of the open door policy brought an end to public control over economic development and seemed to concede the lead in development to foreign capital. Moreover, because the welfare function is so essential to the survival of the regime, Egyptian authorities decided to sacrifice the state development function in order to keep its welfare function. Furthermore, the impact of the open door policy has been in fact commercial, with an emphasis on the search for profit—an objective fully adopted by a bureaucracy eager to exploit public office for personal profit.

The author concludes that the Egyptian bureaucracy is now much less integrated in comprehensive plans for national development. The main preference seems to be for joint venture formulas between the public sector and foreign capital, with the casuality being the Egyptian public sector itself.

In his article on Syria, R. A. Hinnebusch states that under the Asad regime the Syrian bureaucracy has played a central role in agricultural policy and assumed a more technocratic orientation. The bureaucracy's role, however, has been shaped by the Ba'thist ideology and a political structure which gave control over high policy to President Asad and his ruling party. This subordination of agricultural rationality to the calculus of power has led the Syrian regime to use bureaucracy to maximize employment, and to sacrifice profitability to patronage. As a result, agricultural policy planning has been shaped by a collection of goals without rigorous specifications and proper mechanisms for implementation. This problem has been compounded by the failure of the political leadership to give the bureaucracy proper direction, and by the unsettling effects of corruption on the developmental process.

Despite the flaws afflicting the Syrian agrarian apparatus, the author contends that a thorough analysis of actual policy outcomes suggests that the Syrian bureaucracay has put in place and carried out programs of great benefit to agricultural development.

While Hinnebusch's analysis concentrated on the role of the Syrian bureaucracy in agricultural development, J. Jreisat examines the progress Jordan has made toward achieving the goal of national development, and the obstacles that delay modernization efforts. He states that bureaucracy is the major instrument of socio-economic development in Jordan. In carrying out its tasks, however, the Jordanian bureaucracy is hampered by the scarcity of natural resources, by political interference, and by particularistic cultural habits. Moreover, although the Jordanian bureaucracy does not usually attract much criticism, it still suffers from several serious weaknesses: clerkism, centralism, nepotism, and incompentence.

The author concludes that Jordan has experienced major socio-economic change with corresponding intense pressures on government institutions and processes. A number of elements are required for successful change: flexibility and experimentation with innovative administrative processes; revitalization of local authorities and institutions; improvement in the formulation and implementation of public policy; establishment of effective means to gauge the performance of public agencies; and collection of reliable accounting data.

Tawfic Farah explores the success of Kuwait in meeting the challenges of socio-economic and political development. He attributes its political stability, its smooth transition from a subsistence economy to petroleum-induced prosperity, and its success in handling rapid rates of socio-economic change and development to a political culture which permeates the Kuwaiti bureaucracy and intimately bonds Kuwaiti citizens to their ruler. The ruling family had the political insight and necessary management skills to formulate responsive development policies, and the bureaucracy had the will and the commitment to implement them.

Thus, although the Kuwaiti bureaucracy suffers from the same problems one finds in other developing countries, it has succeeded in creating allegiance to the state and in helping the government to maintain prosperity and respond adequately to the needs of Kuwaiti citizens.

Finally, in their article on Algeria, R. Tlemcani and W. W. Hansen analyse the role of the Algerian bureaucracy in development. They explain that the Algerian state owns the significant means of production and has, since independence, used the bureaucracy to implement its statist development model. In doing so, it has emphasized the development of heavy industry and the acquisition of the best available technology to support it. This kind of development edeavour was to take precedence over employment, housing and agricultural development, which were all dependent upon it. Thus in order to reach its developmental goals, the Algerian state's political elite chose to favour rapid economic growth over socio-economic equality and political participation. It also allowed a private sector, deeply articulated with the public sector, to grow in downstream activities. However, one of the main problems with this development model was its failure to create jobs for the bulk of the population. It tended to favour the urban middle classes and skilled workers, and created vast pools of unemployement and underemployment. Furthermore, radical socialist rhetoric aside, this statist development model has given free access to international capital, mainly French and then American, to play a major role in financing Algeria's development strategy. Finally, because of Algeria's reliance on heavy industry, the cost of creating new jobs has been very high.

This state of affairs led to a decline in the living conditions of the labouring classes, the brutalization of the vulnerable and helpless, and the transformation of the labour movement into a state appendage. Although the crisis has been in the making for more than two decades in Algeria, its full impact has been staved off by high oil prices, which allowed the leadership and its bureaucracy to stay in power.

When the oil prices began to drop sharply in the 1980s, the latent crisis became manifest and social unrest began to threaten the legitimacy of the ruling elite, as well as the bureaucracy. This challenge has reduced the role of the state from focusing on development to managing a very difficult economic crisis. The shift of the state focus from development to crisis management was not caused by an incompetent bureaucracy which lacked training and skills. Rather, it was brought about by the high cost of the state's reliance on heavy industry, modern technology transfer and a sharpe decline in oil prices. It is clear that a change of development strategy in Algeria is in order. The state elite and its bureaucracy must come to the conclusion that the statist development model they have been advocating since independence has failed; it must be replaced by a new model which can respond to the needs of the majority of the Algerian population and use to the fullest the talents and skills of its bureaucracy. Failing a new approach to development, the economic crisis will continue and socio-economic and political problems will increase in intensity, threatening the very foundation of the Algerian political system.

It is clear from this discussion that Arab bureaucracies have both strengths and weaknesses. Thus it is important for Arab leaders to follow Ayubi's exhortations and to build upon what Arab bureaucracies do best. It is equally important to realize that like their confreres in other developing countries, Arab bureaucrats have a number of serious problems which constitute major obstacles to development. It is incumbent upon Arab leaders to address these promptly using a new process of socialization which encompasses both the public at large and the bureaucracy. It is hoped that with this dual approach Arab bureaucracies will be stronger in meeting the challenges of socio-economic and political development.

NOTES

1   Abu-Laban, Baha and Sharon McIrvin Abu-Laban, 1986, "Introduction: Development and the Arab World", *Journal of Asian and African Studies* XXI, 1-2, 1-16.
2   Al-Hegelan, Abdelrahman and Monte Palmer, 1985, "Bureaucracy and Development in Saudi Arabia", *The Middle East Journal*, Vol. 39, No. 1, pp. 48-68.
3   Al Nimir, Saud and Monte Palmer, 1982, "Bureaucracy and Development in Saudi Arabia", *Public Administration and Development*, Vol. 2, pp. 93-104.
4   Ayubi, Niziah, N., 1986, "Administrative Development and Development Administration in the Arab World", in Nassir M. Al-Saigh, Ed., *Administrative Reform in the Arab World: Readings*, Amman, Jordan: Arab Organization of Administrative Sciences.
5   Ayubi, Nazih M. N., 1977, Al Thaura Al-Idariyyah (The Administrative Revolution), Cairo: Centre for Political and Strategic Studies, Al-Ahram.
6   El-Fathali, Omar, 1975, "Public Participation and Political Developmental in Libya", Ph.D. dissertation, Florida State University.
7   El-Fathali, Omar and Monte Palmer, 1980, *Political Development and Social Change in Libya*, Lexington, Massachusetts: D. C. Heath, Lexington Books.
8   El-Fathali, Omar and Richard Chackerian, 1983, "Administration: The Forgotten Issue in Arab Development" in Ibrahim Ibrahim, ed., *Arab Resources: The Transformation of a Society*, Washington, D.C.: Centre for Contemporary Arab Studies, pp. 193-209.
9   Iskandar, Adnan, 1964, "The Civil Service of Lebanon", Ph.D. Dissertation, Beirut: The American University of Beirut.
10 Jabbra, Joseph G. and Nancy W. Jabbra, 1983, "Public Service Ethics in the Third World: A Comparative Perspective", in *Ethics in the Public Service*, eds. W. D. Kenneth Kernaghan and O. P. Dwivedi, Brussels: International Institute of Administrative Sciences.
11 Kiserwani, Marun Y., 1971, "Attitudes and Behavior of Lebanese Bureaucrats: A Study in Administrative Corruption", Ph.D. dissertation, Indiana University.
12 Kubursi, Atif A., 1984, *Oil, Industrialization and Development in the Arab Gulf States*, London: Croom Helm.
13 Micaud, Charles, 1969, "Leadership and Development: the Case of Tunisia", *Comparative Politics*, July.
14 Nakib, Khalil and Monte Palmer, 1976, "Traditionalism and Change Among Lebanese Bureaucrats", *International Review of Administrative Sciences* XLII, 1, pp. 15-25.
15 Palmer, Monte and Khalil Nakib, 1978, "Bureaucracy and Development in the Arab World: an Outline for Future Research" in Strategies of Development in the Arab World, International Conference, Louvain, pp. 11-14, December, 1978.
16 Paul, Samuel, 1982, *Managing Development Programs: The Lessons of Success*, Boulder, Colorado: Westview Press.
17 Shuster, James Robert, 1969, "Recruitment and Training in the Moroccan Civil Service", Ph.D. Dissertation, Princeton University.
18 Stephens, Robert, 1976, *The Arabs New Frontier*, Boulder, Colorado: Westview Press.
19 Waterbury, John, 1973, "Endemic and Planned Corruption in Monarchical Regimes", *World Politics*, Vol. 24.
20 Waterbury, John, 1976, "Corruption, Political Stability and Development: Comparative Evidence from Egypt and Morocco", *Government and Opposition*, Vol. 11, No. 4.
21 Zoubi, Abdulla R., 1982, "Toward a Decade of Administrative Development in the Arab World", *Arab Journal of Administration*, April.

Bureaucratic Innovation and Economic Development in the Middle East: A Study of Egypt, Saudi Arabia, and the Sudan

MONTE PALMER[1], ABDELRAHMAN AL-HEGELAN[2],
MOHAMMED BUSHARA ABDELRAHMAN[3], ALI LEILA[4],
EL SAYEED YASSIN[5]

ABSTRACT

Economic policy in the Arab world is dominated by the bureaucracy which plans, co-ordinates, and implements development plans; controls the allocation of the state's natural resources; and is increasingly used by Arab states to regulate the economic activities of their citizens. This paper provides an empirical assessment of bureaucratic innovation and its relationship to economic development in Egypt, Saudi Arabia, and the Sudan. The data are derived from parallel surveys of senior public officials in Sudan and Saudi Arabia, as well as from a general survey of the Egyptian bureaucracy. It concludes that public servants in those countries are not innovative on the job, nor inclined to try new ideas and take risks. Their apathy, which was empirically confirmed by their superiors, does not augur well for economic development in the countries which serve as a focus for this study.

ECONOMIC POLICY IN THE Middle East is dominated by the bureaucracy. This dominance is the result of three specific factors. First, the states of the region rely upon their bureaucracies to plan, co-ordinate, implement, and maintain elaborate economic development plans. Secondly, the states of the region, regardless of their economic and political philosophies, possess large public sector organizations that control, at minimum, the allocation of the state's natural resources. Thirdly, the states of the region have manifested an increasing desire to regulate the economic activities of their citizens.

The dominant position of Middle Eastern bureaucracies in the economic affairs of Middle Eastern states means, in effect, that little progress toward the economic and social develoment of the Middle East is likely to be achieved without the direct and forceful participation of the region's respective

---

1   Florida State University, Tallahassee, FL, U.S.A.
2   Ministry of Finance, Riyadh, Kingdom of Saudi Arabia.
3   Khartoum, Republic of the Sudan.
4   Ein Shams University, Cairo, Egypt.
5   Al Ahram Centre for Political and Strategic Research, Cairo, Egypt.

bureaucratic establishments. This is an unfortunate circumstance, for most states of the region have expressed severe disappointment in the failure of their respective bureaucracies to achieve the developmental goals of the state. Indeed, it has become increasingly apparent that bureaucratic weakness is the Achilles heel of the development process in the region.

The obstacles to enhanced bureaucratic performance in the Middle East appear to be as complex as they are numerous. Any sustained improvement in the performance of Middle Eastern bureaucracies, for example, will ultimately have to address four areas of the bureaucratic endeavor: bureaucratic structure, bureaucratic behavior, bureaucratic interaction with the masses, and bureaucratic interaction with the political and economic environment.[1] Each of the main areas of bureaucratic activity is divided, in turn, into a multitude of sub-areas, the mere delineation of which would require several pages of fine print.

The diverse areas of the bureaucratic process, moreover, are interrelated. Reform in one area is often difficult to achieve without reference to the bureaucratic process as a whole. Organizational and other structural changes in the bureaucracies of the Middle East, for example, have been of limited benefit simply because they were not matched by corresponding changes in bureaucratic behavior. In much the same manner, perennial calls for increased bureaucratic performance have been hamstrung by a myriad of structural and environmental considerations.

The present paper addresses the question of bureaucratic innovation in the Middle East. Innovation, as we use the term, is the willingness to develop and implement new and different approaches to the administrative and social problems of the region.[2] If the bureaucracies of the Middle East cannot or will not provide innovative solutions to the myriad problems of the region, their role in the process of economic and social development will be limited, at best. Moreover, we would stress that innovation is not merely the province of planners at the pinnacle of the bureaucratic structure, but must permeate the entire bureaucratic apparatus. Indeed, critical opportunities for increased productivity and enhanced delivery of services often occur at the lower levels of administration, levels at which contact between the public and the bureaucracy is the greatest.

Objectives

In light of the above discussion, the present paper has two basic objectives. The first objective is to provide an empirical assessment of innovation levels in three diverse Middle Eastern bureaucracies: Egypt, Saudi Arabia, and the Sudan. While the scarcity of bureaucratic innovation in the three states is widely assumed, empirical assessments of the problem do not currently exist. The second objective is to examine various causes of low innovation in Egypt, the Sudan, and Saudi Arabia. In so doing, the paper will address three questions of importance to bureaucratic reform in the Middle East: 1) What measures are required to increase bureaucratic innovation in the region? 2) To what extent is bureaucratic innovation tied to structural and environmental considerations? and 3) Is it possible to speak of a bureaucratic culture common to the region? The latter question addresses the feasibility of technology transfer within the region. Some things do work well in Middle Eastern bureaucracies, and the transfer of bureaucratic technology within the region would surely be easier than the borrowing of bureaucratic technology from the radically different political and social environments of the United States, Western Europe, or the Soviet Union.

Egypt, Saudi Arabia, and the Sudan, it should be noted, have three distinct bureaucratic histories. Egypt possesses the world's most venerable bureaucratic traditions, traditions that return, at least in theory, to the days of the Pharaohs. More realistically, the modern Egyptian civil service finds its origins in the era of Mohammed Ali.[3] The Sudan, for its part, was administered largely by British Civil Servants until 1956.[4] With the granting of Sudanese independence in that year, the vast majority of the British expatriates returned to England, leaving the new state to shift for itself. Saudi Arabia, in turn, presents yet a third model of administrative development. Possessing little more than the bare bones of an administrative structure in the mid-1950's, the Arabian kingdom would soon be overwhelmed by an era of wealth and economic prosperity.[5] The Saudi bureaucracy simple exploded in a frantic effort to keep pace with the demands of an oil economy. Even today, a high percentage of its personnel continue to be drawn from Egypt, Palestine, and other neighboring states possessing a deeper bureaucratic tradition.

Environmental differences between the three states are also marked. Egypt, the most populous of the Arab states, is also among the poorest. Saudi Arabia, by contrast, is the richest state of the region, yet remains severely underpopulated. The Sudan, though possessing a substantial population, is beset by grinding poverty and communal conflict. Egypt is an urban-oriented society that has long been exposed to the forces of education and Westernization. The Sudan and Saudi Arabia have been far less exposed to the forces of Westernization. This situation, however, is changing rapidly. The political system of Saudi Arabia has been marked by stability and continuity. Egypt has experienced various political transformations, yet has maintained a continuity of regime for more than three decades. The Sudan has suffered manifest political instability. Egypt and the Sudan have both experimented with various forms of state socialism. Both currently possess mixed economies. Saudi Arabia is capitalist in orientation, yet the state is the repository of the nation's vast wealth and plays a dominant role in most phases of economic activity.

As the bureaucratic development of the three states has been shaped by markedly different historical and social circumstances, one might expect substantial differences in their bureaucratic behavior. Countering this expectation, however, is the similarity of Arabic and Islamic culture that pervades the Middle East as a cultural entity. To be considered also, is the pervasive influence of Egypt in the region as a whole and on Saudi Arabia and the Sudan in particular. Egyptian media dominated the Middle East. Egyptian civil servants have played a major role in shaping and staffing the Saudi bureaucracy. Egypt historically claimed the Sudan as a part of Egyptian territory. The roots of Egyptian influences in the Sudan are deep, indeed. Perhaps the diversity which characterizes the three states is less important in shaping the behavior of their respective bureaucrats than the force of Arabian culture and the pervasive influence of Egyptian values.

Methodology

The data presented in this paper are based upon parallel surveys of senior officials in the Sudan and Saudi Arabia, as well as a general survey of the Egyptian bureaucracy, including senior officials, that incorporated many of the questionnaire items utilized in the Saudi and Sudanese surveys.

The Egyptian survey was based upon a random sample of 825 Egyptian civil servants and was conducted by the Al Ahram Center for Political and Strategic Studies during the late spring of 1983. The sample was selected in relatively equal proportions from the Ministry of Social Affairs, the Ministry of Industry, and the Aluminium Corporation. The sample was stratified to reflect senior (n = 156), middle (n = 321), and lower (319) levels of the bureaucracy. The questionnaires were administered as direct interviews, with thirty questionnaires being deleted from the sample as a result of excessive non-responses or technical problems.

The Sudanese survey was based upon the distribution of 400 questionnaires to senior officials in eight central ministries and three public corporations in the Khartoum area. Fifty-one percent (n = 205) were returned, representing 40% of the senior officials in the Khartoum area.

The Saudi survey of senior officials was based upon the distribution of 231 questionnaires to the total population of senior officials (top five levels) in the Ministries of Finance, Agriculture, Health, Information, Civil Services, Commerce, Industry and Higher Education in the Riyadh area, resulting in a return rate of fifty-three percent (n = 123).

Reliability in the three studies was ascertained by comparing response patterns among similar items as well as by matching reponse patterns with established characteristics of the bureaucracy. Inconsistent response rates in the three studies were less than five percent, with little discernible evidence of response bias among similar items with inverted response selections.

The Egyptian questionnaires was designed in the Arabic language by a five-member team of researchers at the Center. The original questionnaire was pre-tested utilizing a sample of 70 officials reflecting all employment levels. The questionnaire averaged approximately 130 questions in length, with separate versions of the questionnaire being administered to each of the three administrative levels. Approximately 75% of the questionnaire items were uniform across the three levels, with the remaining 25% of the items being tailored to the specific circumstances of each level. The questionnaire was

administered by a specially trained team of graduate students from the Department of Sociology at Ein Shams University.

The Sudanese and Saudi questionnaires were administered in 1983 by Dr.
Mohammed Abdul Rahman Al Bushira and Dr. Abdelrahman Rahman Al
Hegelan respectively. Both questionnaires were extensively pre-tested.

Assessing Bureaucratic Innovation

Assessing the innovation levels of bureaucrats in the three states involved
two steps. First, senior bureaucrats in each of the three states were requested
to assess the level of innovation among their subordinates. Secondly, the senior
bureaucrats in question were asked a series of questions designed to reflect
their own predispositions toward innovation as it pertained to social change
and development planning. The two assessments are clearly linked, for it is
unlikely that senior officials predisposed against social change will instill the
desire for innovation in their subordinates.

Table 1

Assessments of Bureaucratic Innovation

What is the percentage of your subordinates who attempt to innovate or try new ideas?

	Saudi	Egypt	Sudan
0-10%	41.9	61.2	55.6
11-25	29.1	19.7	25.9
26-50	16.2	13.2	10.7
51-100	12.8	5.0	7.9
	100%	100%	100%
Non-response 6		4	0

The assessments of subordinate innovation levels appear in Table 1. As
was to be anticipated from the existing literature, the number of employees
willing to try new ideas—a particularly broad definition of innovation—was
very low.[6] Arab bureaucrats are clearly not predisposed to try new ideas, a
situation that must be altered if Arab bureaucracies are to play a dynamic role
in the development process.

If senior bureaucrats score their subordinates low in terms of innovation,
how willing are they, themselves, to pursue innovative programs. In order to
answer this question, the respondents were asked a series of questions designed
to measure their willingness to embark upon development programs that might
involve social and cultural changes in their respective societies. The items
focused on social and cultural change, for it is truly difficult to imagine

Table 2

Predispositions Toward Developmental Innovation

		Egypt	Saudi	Sudan
It is best to cancel or change programs that could cause social conflict				
	Yes	87.8	89.2	68.3
	No	12.2	10.8	31.7
Social change should not be instituted at the expense of traditional values				
	Yes	67.1	94.9	84.3
	No	32.9	5.1	15.7
Economic development should be pursued even if it means hardship for the majority of the people				
	Yes	53.2	62.3	53.0
	No	46.8	37.7	47.0

economic and social development programs that do not involve at least a modicum of social change and stress. Specifically, the questionnaire items presented in Table 2 address three specific issues: 1) social conflict, 2) social values, and 3) imposing economic hardship for the sake of development. While the weight of all responses tended to be on the side of preserving the status quo, the respondents as a whole were least distressed by the prospect of imposing economic burdens upon their respective populations for the sake of greater economic development. Indeed, economic hardship was the only area in which a majority of the respondents indicated a predisposition toward developmental innovation. The imposition of economic hardship, it seems, carries far less risk than programs that might exacerbate social conflict or threaten established values. An overwhelming majority of all respondents indicated a marked reluctance to venture into areas that might challenge social values, a figure that reached the 95% level in Saudi Arabia and 84% in the Sudan. In much the same manner, an overwhelming majority of all respondents were predisposed against programs that might generate social conflict, a figure that topped the 85% level in both Egypt and Saudi Arabia.

While respondents in all three states were predisposed against change-oriented programs, it is interesting to note the substantial differences that occurred between the three samples. The Saudis were clearly the most reluctant to initiate any programs that might result in value change or social conflict. The Egyptians, having experienced the socialist programs of the Nasser era, were far more willing than either the Saudis or the Sudanese to attack traditional values. The Egyptians, however, were extremely concerned about social conflict. The Sudanese, by contrast, were very conderned about preserving traditional values, but were somewhat less concerned about the threat of social conflict. This circumstance may well reflect the fact that the Sudanese have lived with social conflict throughout the period of their independence.

Taken as a whole, the results indicate that 84% of respondents in each of the three samples found at least one reason to avoid social innovation. The mean non-innovative score for the three items suggest that 70% of the Egyptians, 68% of the Sudanese, and 82% of the Saudis were predisposed against developmental innovation. If the less burdensome economic hardship item is removed from the equation, the percentage of senior officials predisposed against developmental innovation jumps to 78%, 77%, and 92% respectively.

Explanations of Low Bureaucratic Innovation in the Middle East

The first step in improving levels of innovation among Middle Eastern civil servants is to understand the causes of their reluctance to innovate. In attempting this endeavor, we shall examine two types of explanations: scholarly explanations and practitioner explanations. By scholarly explanations we refer to the explanations provided by scholars who have attempted to fathom the problems of the bureaucracy from the outside. These explanations tend to be heavily social-psychological in nature. Practitioner explanations, by contrast, focus on the practical experience of the senior officials surveyed. The former benefit from the body of social, developmental, and administrative theory that has been generated over the past several decades and that drawn upon a universal base of experience. The latter draws upon the experience of individuals intimately familiar with the daily workings of their respective bureaucracies. There is no way to indicate which of the two points of view is the more valid. Quite clearly, the more they converge, the closer to the heart of the problem one is likely to be.

For analytical purposes, the explanations of low bureaucratic innovativeness will be divided into five categories: 1) systemic explanations, 2) cultural/personal explanations, 3) insecurity related explanations, 4) group dynamic explanations, and 5) supervisor dynamic explanations.

Structural problems constitute the most visible and, consequently, the most analyzed dimension of the bureaucratic process in the Arab world. Foremost among the structural influences upon innovation is the question of salaries. Government salaries in Egypt and the Sudan are pathetically low. In Egypt, government salaries no longer provide government employees with an adequate standard of living. No less than 85% of our Egyptian sample, for example, found it necessary to supplement their positions with secondary employment. Even more problematic is the growing gap in wages between the public and private sectors of the Egyptian economy. Not only are the wages of Egyptian civil servants low in absolute terms, but they are also low in relative terms. While Egyptian civil servants struggle to make ends meet, their counterparts in the newly-revitalized private sector are living in comparative splendor. Civil servants in Saudi Arabia are not underpaid in absolute terms or in comparison to their Egyptian and Sudanese counterparts. They are, however, severely underpaid in relation to the Saudi private sector. Indeed, one of the major problems facing the Saudi bureaucracy is the migration of its more dynamic employees to the private sector.

Salaries and related incentives such as promotions and bonuses, needless to say, are central to the question of innovation. Simply stated, poorly paid employees have little incentive to try new ideas or to take unnessary risks.

A second set of structural problems, related to bureaucratic innovation in the Middle East, centers on both the low skill levels of government employees and the inadequate use of those skills that are available. To fully understand this situation, it must be noted that each of the three states under consideration utilizes bureaucratic staffing as a means of providing mass employment. In Egypt, for example, all university graduates are guaranteed a bureaucratic position regardless of their qualifications. The Egyptian government, in addition to its concern for the welfare of its population, does not want to contend with the political volatility of widespread intellectual unemployment. In Saudi Arabia, government employment serves as one of the primary mechanisms for providing an equitable distribution of the state's bountiful oil revenues to all strata of the Saudi population.

Welfare-oriented staffing policies influence bureaucratic apathy in three ways. First, welfare-based recruitment draws large numbers of poorly-skilled individuals into the bureaucracy. Having low skill levels to begin with, they are poorly qualified to perform a wide range of tasks. Moreover, their low skill levels tend to make them insecure and reluctant to attempt tasks that will amplify their inadequacies and perhaps render them vulnerable to dismissal or disciplinary action. Regardless of predispositions toward innovation, poorly-skilled individuals are not well positioned to engage in innovative behavior. Secondly, welfare-based recruitment leads to overstaffing and to the misallocation of those skills that are available. Misplaced skills are of little more utility than no skills at all. Thirdly, welfare-based recruitment creates an environment of non-competitive complacency. Government positions tend to be looked upon as a fiefdom, as something the recipient is entitled to by divine right. Competition breeds innovation; conformity stifles it.

Salary levels and skills are but two of the most obvious structural impediments to bureaucratic innovation in the Middle East. Many Middle Eastern bureaucrats lack the authority to execute all but the most routine tasks, a situation exacerbated by the tendency of supervisory officials to concentrate as much authority as possible in their own hands.[7] Nor is the situation eased by the morass of bureaucratic regulations and overlapping authority patterns that characterize Middle Eastern bureaucracies. Many Middle East officials are sincerely confused about their responsibilities; others use ambiguous rules as a pretext for avoiding work or dodging responsibility. Either way, innovation suffers. Also, it should be noted that bureaucratic regulations in the Middle East focus on sins of commission rather than sins of omission. It is far more dangerous to stick one's neck out than it is to do nothing.

Given the clear link between structural problems and low bureaucratic innovation, one might well be tempted to explain the apathy of Middle Eastern bureaucrats solely on structural grounds. Such a conclusion, if valid, would mean that innovation could be substantially increased simply by means of structural reform. Indeed, salary increases, of themselves, might alleviate a lion's share of the problem.

Such optimism, unfortunately, appears to be premature. While there can be little doubt that structural problems do have a debilitating impact on innovation, there is little evidence to suggest that increased salaries or other structural reforms will, of themselves, increase innovation or motivation. Structural improvements may make it easier for workers to perform at a comfortable level, but such improvements are unlikely to push them beyond that level. This point has long been associated with the work of Frederick Herzberg.[8] Based upon a detailed analysis of the sources of job satisfaction and job dissatisfaction reported in 12 diverse studies possessing a combined sample of 1,685 respondents representing a wide variety of occupations and cultures, Herzberg concluded that employees responded to two diverse types of stimuli: hygienic stimuli and motivational stimuli. Hygienic stimuli are basically structural in nature and include salary structure, work conditions, and job security. Hygienic stimuli, according to Herzberg, are essentially negative. They are the primary source of worker complaints and tend to depress performance if they fall below reasonable levels. Improving the hygienic environment, as suggested above, will improve productivity only to the point at which adverse hygienic factors no longer serve as a depressant.

Herzberg's motivational stimuli, by contrast, focus upon opportunities for achievement, recognition, and personal growth. As positive stimuli and by building upon the need for growth and recogniton, motivational stimuli provide the basis for increasing employee effort, for stimulating employees to go beyond existing norms.

Herzberg's theory, if correct, would deal a severe blow to the hopes of those who feel that improving bureaucratic innovation in the Middle East is merely a matter of improving salary structures and of alleviating the various structural problems surveyed above.

In summarizing the influence of structural variables upon bureaucratic innovation in the Middle East, then, it would seem logical to conclude that structural circumstances must be substantially improved in order to eliminate their negative impact on innovation. One must also conclude, however, that structural improvements are not sufficient, of themselves, to solve the problem of low innovation. One must probe deeper into the sources of bureaucratic behavior.

The cultural impediments to innovation find their origins in the attitudes and predispositions that government officials bring to their work. In this regard, the sociological and psychological literature is replete with explanations of why Middle Eastern officials should be less than innovative in solving the problems of their region. Topping the list of cultural explanations is the sense of fatalism that tends to pervade many Middle Eastern societies. If the affairs of man are regulated by God, the need for human innovative is minimal.[9] Related theories suggest that Middle Eastern societies place a special emphasis on social conformity.[10] Early socialization patterns reward conformity. They do little to reinforce creativity. Yet a third set of social theories stresses the poorly-developed sense of work ethic or achievement motivation in many Middle Eastern societies.[11] According to this view, selfesteem in Middle Eastern societies is not necessarily tied to levels of material achievement. Middle Easterners, accordingly, are less likely than their Western counterparts to be driven by an internalized need for achievement. As innovation is one path to greater achievement, Middle Easterners are also less likely to innovate than are their Western counterparts. Finally, it might also be suggested that most Middle Eastern societies place greater emphasis on traditional values than do many Western societies. The past is to be valued. It is not to be discarded lightly. Change is not perceived as an unmitigated good. Social continuity rivals the desire for modernity and change.

It would be difficult to suggest that each of the above forces and their variants are equally applicable across the full spectrum of Middle Eastern cultures. Nevertheless, sufficient literature on the topic exists to suggest that these themes, collectively, should provide a cultural bias against bureaucratic innovation. This is an important point, for cultural obstacles to bureaucratic innovation may be far more difficult to alter than structural obstacles to innovation. Indeed, cultural biases against innovation could well undermine structural alterations designed to increase innovation.

If cultural influences predispose the Middle Eastern bureaucrat to be non-innovative, those predispositions are clearly reinforced by the group dynamics in the work environment.[12] Innovative individuals—and there are innovative individuals in Middle Eastern bureaucracies—find their suggestions for change squelched by peers resentful of the disruptions that innovative changes bring to their routine or jealous of the attemption that accrues to the innovator. Innovation in a hostile group environment is an uphill battle. It is a battle that must be fought by more than a handful of individuals, and it is a battle that must be reinforced by supervisors at all levels.

Innovation levels in Middle Eastern bureaucracies are also depressed by what Berger termed the security consciousness of Middle Eastern bureaucracies.[13] A bureaucratic position in the Middle East tends to be a sinecure; a base that provides its occupant with a stable salary, access to government circles, at least minimal respect, and a very tolerable work load. Few Middle Eastern bureaucrats, according to Ayubi, are willing to jeopardize such a pleasing state of affairs by rocking the boat.[14] To quote an Egyptian proverb, "The more you work, the more errors you make." The same principle applies to innovation. One might also recall the earlier observation that the insecurity of many Middle Eastern bureaucrats is heightened by inadequate skill levels.

Finally, non-innovative tendencies in Middle Eastern bureaucracies are reinforced by the process of supervisor dynamics. Supervisors in the Midlle

East tend to concentrate as much authority as possible in their own hands.[15] Little authority is delegated. Subordinates receive little positive reinforcement for work well done. Innovation and risk-taking are not reinforced. Many supervisory personnel in the Middle East prefer subordinates who keep a low profile and who don't "rock the boat". Subservience often brings greater rewards than hard work.

Explanations of Bureaucratic Apathy by Senior Officials

The manner in which senior officials view the problem of bureaucratic innovation is critically important for three basic reasons. First, and perhaps foremost, senior officials are those individuals directly responsible for initiating programs designed to increase worker innovation. Supervisors are far more likely to attack the problems they believe cause low innovation than they are to implement programs of a theoretical nature suggested by outsiders. Secondly, senior officials are those individuals closest to the problem. Their opinions on the subject must be respected. Indeed, their perceptions may well be closer to the mark than the views of outside experts. Thirdly, explanations of low innovation cited by both external experts and supervisory personnel are likely to be more accurate than the explanations cited by either the theorist or the practitioner alone.

Assessing the manner in which senior officials view the problem of low innovation was approched in two ways. First, senior bureaucrats were asked to evaluate the importance of each of the theoretical explanations of low innovation discussed above. Secondly, they were requested to indicate what they felt to be the first and second most important causes of low innovation among their subordinates.

The results of the battery of questionnaire items asking respondents to evaluate the relevance of each of the diverse explanations of low innovation suggested by the theoretical literature are presented in Tables 3 and 4. Table 3 contains two types of data: 1) the percentage of respondents who felt that the explanation in question was "very important" and 2) the percentage score of the respondents who felt the explanation in question to be either "very important" or "important." The latter column is labeled "relevant." The data for the "most important" explanation of low innovation appears in Table 4. It should be noted that the Egyptian questionnaire contained only the first set of questions.

The first and most important conclusion to be reached from the data presented in Table 3 is that all of the explanations suggested by the theoretical literature were considered relevant by a large number of senior officials in each of the three countries under consideration. This finding, of itself, indicates a high level of congruity between the theoretical literature and the evaluations of the senior officials. In so doing, it also suggests 1) that senior officials are cognizant of the broader cultural and personality dimensions of the innovation problem, and 2) that efforts to overcome the problem of low innovation may

Table 3

Explanations of Low Bureaucratic Innovation

	Egypt		Saudi		Sudan	
Systemic	VI*	R*	VI	R	VI	R
Low skills	63.6%	96.1%	57.3%	93.2%	73.5%	93.6%
Low incentives	70.8	94.2	44.8	76.7	69.8	90.7
Culture						
Low concern for job	29.4	78.4	17.1	52.3	55.0	84.7
Cultural bias	12.2	43.2	8.0	33.9	29.7	65.3
Risk/Security						
Avoid responsibility	21.8	73.5	15.9	56.6	26.5	64.7
Fear mistakes	26.4	79.1	14.9	58.8	22.5	60.3
Group Dynamics						
Upset colleagues	8.5	43.8	20.2	47.4	16.3	48.8
No one else works	29.1	66.2	11.5	47.8˙	21.8	56.4
Supervisor Dynamics						
Fear supervisor	28.4	58.1	20.0	53.0	26.3	54.1
Lack authority	36.2	79.2	19.1	57.3	36.9	72.9

* VI = Percent "Very Important". R = Percent "Relevant" (Very important + important).

Table 4

Most Important Explanations of Low Innovation

	Sudan		Saudi	
	1st	1st & 2nd	1st	1st & 2nd
Systemic				
Low skills	53.2%	58.1	44.6%	59.8
Low incentives	13.2	48.0	13.9	41.1
Culture				
General apathy	10.7	29.8	4.0	7.3
Cultural bias	1.5	5.9	3.0	5.5
No feel for problem	—	—	6.9	16.7
Risk/Security				
Avoid responsibility	4.4	10.3	9.9	22.9
Year of mistakes	2.0	6.4	3.0	6.3
Group Dynamics				
No one else does	1.5	7.4	—	—
Upset peers	1.0	4.9	—	6.5
Supervisor Dynamics				
Lack authority	6.8	16.6	5.0	13.7
Fear supervisor	5.4	11.8	9.9	20.8
	100%		100%	

x

be complex indeed. This being the case, it is unlikely that the problem of low bureaucratic innovation will be solved merely by structural adjustments or other "quick fixes." Considerations of culture, group dynamics, and supervisor dynamics must all be incorporated into programs designed to increase bureaucratic innovation.

Having noted a general awareness of the complexity of the innovation problem, it must also be noted that senior officials in each of the three states attributed a lion's share of the problem to the low qualifications of their subordinates and the lack of adequate incentives. In the view of more than 90% of the combined sample, their subordinates were simply unqualified to innovate. The distance between structural and behavioral explanations is particularly striking in Table 4.

Though not rivalling skill levels in terms of importance, it was interesting to note the prominence of subordinate insecurity as an obstacle to greater innovation. A majority of all the officials surveyed, and more than 70% of the Egyptian officials indicated that their subordinates were afraid of making mistakes that would leave them vulnerable to disciplinary action. This fear is also manifest in parallel results indicating that subordinate officials were reluctant to assume added responsibilities.[16] Innovation, by its nature requires risk taking and the assumption of responsibility.

The climate of insecurity that pervades Middle Eastern bureaucracies must ultimately find at least part of its cause in the climate of relations between supervisors and subordinates. As reported elsewhere, senior officials in the Middle East manifest a strong desire to concentrate as much authority as possible in their own hands.[17] They are not prone to delegate authority, and they do worry about the misuse of authority by their subordinates. It should not be surprising then, that a clear majority of senior officials, in each of the three countries, indicated that innovative tendencies were depressed by "fear of upsetting the supervisor." They also indicated that their employees lacked authority to innovate, a matter that could easily be remedied by the senior officials if they so desired. Both results suggest that the climate of supervisor/subordinate relations does little to promote innovation.

Cultural and psychological explanations were also perceived as relevant to the innovation problem. The major emphasis, however, was placed upon the "general disinterest of subordinates in their work" rather than upon a cultural bias against innovation. The same theme is reflected in the results of the group dynamics items, items which reflect a severe moral problem among Middle Eastern bureaucrats.

In spite of broad areas of similarity between the three samples, Saudi officials placed far less emphasis on lack of incentives as a cause of low innovation than did their counterparts from Egypt and the Sudan. This ranking reflects the greater wealth of Saudi Arabia and the fact that bureaucratic compensation in Saudi Arabia is more than adequate to provide government officials with a reasonable standard of living. This clearly is not the case in Egypt and the Sudan. In Egypt and the Sudan, the salary/incentive structure is so low as to depress performances. According to Herzberg's and related theories, an increase of salaries in Egypt and the Sudan might increase productivity at least minimally by removing the negative influence of Herzberg's hygienic facors. Such increases in productivity—and by inference, innovation— would be minimal and would level off at the point at which the hygienic environment became tolerable. Moreover, merely increasing salaries can do little to alleviate the negative impact of insecurity on innovation. Further innovation would require incentives of a positive nature. In Saudi Arabia, by contrast, current salary and incentive levels are clearly adequate. Salary levels do not depress performance. What is lacking are Herzberg's positive motivators. Indeed, informal conversations with Saudi officials indicate that one of their major problems is devising non-monetary incentives that will enable them to retain their more productive people. For ambitious Saudis, money is not a problem. There is simply too much money available for those willing to work. Reflecting this state of affairs, senior officials in Saudi Arabia placed somewhat greater emphasis on subordinate insecurity and supervisor dynamics than did their Egyptian and Sudanese counterparts. This difference in emphasis is evident in both Tables 3 and 4. The contrast between the Saudis on the one hand and the Egyptians and the Sudanese on the other vis-à-vis the question of the concentration of authority is even more pronounced in relation to worker apathy—a clear correlate of low innovation, and has been discussed at length elsewhere.[18] One might note in passing that the intense concentration of authority by senior Saudi officials, when combined with their considerable adversion to developmental innovation, suggests that senior officials in Saudi Arabia are ill-disposed to generate innovation among their subordinates. Support for this proposition is to be found in a decision-making item contained in the Saudi and Sudanese questionnaires in which respondents were asked to express their level of agreement with the proposition that, "One should be cautious in making even routine decisions." Eighty-six percent of the Saudi officials answered in the affirmative as opposed to 68% of the Sudanese officials.

In summary, the major cross cultural differences in approaches to bureaucratic innovation centered on the economic dimension. Egyptian and Sudanese officials, because of the low wage structure in their respective states, were somewhat more predisposed than their Saudi counterparts to view low innovation as a problem of incentives. This logic, if valid, would suggest that increases in wages would lead to an increase in innovation. The Saudi's, while finding incentives a problem, placed special focus upon relations between supervisors and subordinates. The Saudi experience is of particular interest for it supports the Herzberg hypothesis that the mere provision of an adequate wage will not, of itself, stimulate innovation. An adequate wage may be a necessary condition for productivity but, as the Saudi experience demonstrates, it is clearly not a sufficient condition. Monetary incentives alone are unlikely to solve the problem of low innovation unless they are combined with programs that address all of the relevant dimensions of bureaucratic behavior.

Clear, cross-cultural differences also emerged in regard to the innovativeness of the senior officials in the three states. While approximately 75% of the Egyptian and Sudanese respondents were predisposed against developmental programs that might engender social conflict or value change, the figure jumps to 92% among the Saudis. Explanation of the greater conservatism of the Saudis is not difficult to come by. Saudi Arabia has been far less exposed to Western influences that Egypt. It has also avoided the social conflict endemic to the Sudan. Economically, the Saudis face less pressure to engage in radical development programs. The Egyptians and the Sudanese have far less choice in the matter. Politically, Saudi Arabia is the protector of Islam. Traditional values must be preserved. To do otherwise would be heresy. Senior Saudi administrators clearly see their role as one of preserving traditional values.

In examining the question of a uniform bureaucratic culture across the three states, one encounters something of a quandary. The behavior of the Saudis clearly varies from that of the Egyptians and the Sudanese. This variance, however, appears to be explained largely by economic considerations. At the same time, it is difficult to ignore culture continuities in the responses of the three samples. All three samples emphasize structural problems as the major obstacles to innovation. All acknowledged the insecurity of their subordinates. All downplayed suggestions of a cultural bias toward innovation. Clearly, their explanations of low innovation contained broad areas of agreement. How, then, are the developmental predispositions of the senior officials best interpreted? Does one stress the greater conservatism of the Saudi? Or, is the proper focus placed upon the substantial conservatism (low predisposition toward innovation) of the Egyptians and the Sudanese in spite of their greater exposure to Western influences and their pressing economic problems? The Egyptians and the Sudanese are more willing to accept social innovation than the Saudis, but are they willing enough to take the measures required to make their respective economies economically viable?

NOTES

1   For a review of material on this topic see: Ferrel Heady, *Public Administration: A Comparative Perspective* 2nd ed. (New York: Marcel Dekker, 1979) Earlier works included Fred W. Riggs, ed., *Frontiers of Development Administration* (Durham, N.C.: Duke University Press, 1970); Ralph Braibanti, ed., *Political and Administrative Development* (Durham, N.C.: Duke University Press, 1969); Joseph LaPalombara, ed. *Bureaucracy and Political Development: Politics, Administration and Change* (New York: McGraw Hill, 1966); Lee Sigelman, "In Search of Comparative Administration," Public Administration Group (American Society for Public Administration, 1964); Jong Jun, "Renewing the Study of Comparative Administration: Some Reflections on the Current Possibilities," *Public Administration Review* Vol. 36, No. 6 (1976): 641-647; Krishna K. Tummala, ed., *Administrative Systems Abroad* (Washington, D.C.: University Press of America, 1982).
2   Victor A. Thompson, *Bureaucracy and Innovation* (Tuskaloosa, Alabama: University of Alabama Press, 1969).

3 Nazih Ayubi, *Bureaucracy and Politics in Contemporary Egypt* (London: Ithaca Press, 1980); Samir M. Youssef, *System of Management in Egyptian Public Enterprises* (Cairo, Center for Middle East Management Studies, The American University in Cairo, 1983, pp. 26-27).

4 Peter K. Bechtold, *Politics in the Sudan* (New York: Praeger Publishers, 1976).

5 Fatima Amin Shaker, "Modernization of the Developing Nations: A Case of Saudi Arabia" (Doctoral Dissertation, Purdue University, 1972).

6 El Sayeed Yassin, Monte Palmer, Ali Laila, "Innovation and Development: The Case of the Egyptian Bureaucracy," (Paper presented at the Convention of the Middle East Studies Association, 1984).

7 Monte Palmer, Abdul Rahman Al Hegelan and Mohammed Bushara Abdulrahman, "Bureaucratic Rigidity and Economic Development in The Middle East: A Study of Egypt, the Sudan and Saudi Arabia," (Paper presented at the Convention of the Middle East Studies Association of North America, New Orleans, 1986).

8 Frederick Herzberg, *The Managerial Choice* (Homewood, Ill.: Dow Jones-Irwin, 1976). See Chapter 2.

9 Sania Hamady, *Temperament and Character of the Arabs* (New York: Twayne Publishers, 1960).

10 Ernest Gellner, "The Tribal Society and its Enemies," in *The Conflict of Tribe and State*, ed. Richard Tapper (London: Croom Helm). Ernest Gellner, *Muslim Society* (London: Cambridge University Press, 1981).

11 D. C. McClelland, *The Achieving Society* (Princeton, N.J.: Van Nostrand, 1961).

12 Victor A. Thompson, *Bureaucracy and Innovation.*

13 Morroe Berger, *Bureaucracy and Society in Egypt* (Princeton, N.J.: Princeton University Press, 1957).

14 Nazih Ayubi, "Bureaucracies: Expanding Size, Changing Roles" (Paper presented before the International Conference on State, Nation and Integration in the Arab World, Corfu, 1-6 September, 1984).

15 Palmer, Al Hegelan, Bushara, "Bureaucratic Rigidity and Economic Development."

16 *Ibid.*

17 *Ibid.*

18 *Ibid.*

Bureaucracy and Development in the Sudan

MUKHTAR AL ASSAM

University of the United Arab Emirats, Al Ain, United Arab Emirates

ABSTRACT

With good education and a relatively high functional capability, Sudanese Public servants have had the potential to play a major role in the political and socio-economic development of their country. Unfortunately, all development plans since independence have failed to achieve their goals. This failure was caused by administrative inefficiency and obsolete structures, bureaucratic infighting, and the lack of co-ordination, leading to poor implemention and execution of government policies.

Introduction

IN THIS PAPER AN EFFORT will be made to analyze the role of bureaucracy in the socio-economic and political development of Sudan. The word "bureaucracy" is used here to refer to all hierarchical organization-serving staffs; thus Sudanese bureaucracy includes regular ministries, directorates, departments, and public corporations as well as the military and police. The word "development" has acquired several meanings: it suggests for some, economic growth and industrialization; for others, nation building, social justice, and popular participation and representation. Some scholars distinguish the notion from those of progress and economic growth; for them, development serves as a framework that transforms progress in particular respects into overall social progress.[1] Riggs and Waldo define development as "the movement toward the freedom to choose goals and the ability to realize them".[2] However, it is not intended here to enter into definitional problems surrounding the term. Development can be taken to refer to all of the above notions. We are concerned here with the role played by the bureaucracy in the socio-economic and political development of the country.

Bureaucracy and political development are sustaining a running debate among the scholars over whether bureaucracy plays an essentially positive role, facilitating political development in the sense of promoting conciliar government structures on the one hand, and socio-economic modernization on the other; or whether it has a negative impact, restricting the growth and development of representative institutions.[3] This question will be dealt with in the third section of this paper. In the Sudan, the bureaucratic sector enjoys better

education and possesses a relatively high functional capability and high relevance to socio-economic development; it has gained an overwhelming degree
of influence over government policy as representative institutional structures
(legislatures and parties) are weak and fragile. It will be argued that the all-
powerful Sudanese bureaucracy hampers the development of representative
institutions. It will be pointed out that there is a grave developmental
imbalance between bureaucracy and representative institutions with the
former being better developed and more powerful than the conciliar structures
of government, e.g., political parties, parliaments, and local government
legislative bodies. The Sudanese experience, in this respect, supports the
arguments of social scientists and writers like La Palombara, Riggs, Heady,
and Eisenstadt.

In the Sudan, as well as in many less-developed countries, the government
is seen as a "prime mover". It is not only responsible for creating basic order
and keeping peace but also for initiating and executing long-term development
and change. It is considered to be the principal agent of development. The
Sudan has had a long tradition of active state participation in the economy.
Before independence, some of the main state economic enterprises had been
the Gezira Scheme in central Sudan, which was founded in 1925 for pump-
irrigated cotton cultivation, and the Zande Scheme of southern Sudan, which
combined both agriculture and textiles. By 1969 almost one million farmers
and their families, as well as many casual workers from the western part of the
country, derived their livelihood directly from the former. Further enhancing
the role of the state in the economy were the extensive nationalizations of 1970
which led the state to assume additional economic activities,[4]

However, there has been an ever-widening gap between the rising expectations of the Sudanese people and the real achievements. To put it in another
way there is little relationship between plans and their implementations. When
development plans are drawn up, many people expect immediate results and
even miracles. Consequently, the gap between the "revolution of rising expectations" and achievement leads to the revolution of "rising frustrations" and
growing dissatisfaction.[5]

The role of bureaucracy in the socio-economic development of the Sudan
will be dealt with under a separate sub-heading in the last section of this paper.

It is noted that almost all of the socio-economic plans, since independence,
failed to achieve their goals. Poor implementation and execution of plans was
attributed to administrative inefficiency and inherited, obsolete administrative
setups. Several administrative reforms were carried out in attempts to overcome these inadequacies. Such reforms will be discussed and analyzed in this
work.

Sudanese Bureaucracy

In the contemporary political and administrative history of the Sudan, five
distinct eras can be noted:

1. From 1954 to 1958, the first multi-party system and parliamentary government;
2. From 1958 to 1964, the first military government of General Abboud;
3. From 1964 to 1969, the October popular uprising and the second multi-party system and parliamentary government;
4. From 1969 to 1985, the second military government of General Nimeiri and the presidential system; and,
5. From 1985 until now (1989), the April popular uprising, the transitional government, and the third multi-party system and parliamentary government.

It is evident from this chronological account that the Sudan has moved in a cycle from a parliamentary government to a military government, then with the latter defeated by a popular uprising, back to a parliamentary government and so on. The Sudan is probably the only country that has witnessed two popular uprisings in less than two decades, both of which managed to overthrow military regimes with the help of the bureaucracy.

Some of the salient features of these eras are worth mentioning. During the first period the colonial public service was semi-military; Governors of Provinces, Local Government Officers and Health Officers were dressed in khaki uniforms and wore military stripes on their shoulders. Today's official uniform for Local Government Officers and Inspectors reflects those military traditions. In 1956, the Sudan was declared an independent state, thus ending the Anglo-Egyptian Condominium rule and bringing to an end a long political debate over unity with Egypt. Also this period witnessed the rapid Sudanization of the public service.

The second and third parliamentary government eras are characterized by the revival of the political parties, the most important of which are the Umma and the Unionist Democratic Parties. Both parties have little or no concern with ideology and neither is aggressive in the pursuit of economic development and modernization. Both parties advocate a "mixed" type economy and are pro-Western. Almost all of the parliamentary governments in the Sudan are formed by coalitions of these two parties.

A Governmental Commission in 1968 calculated that between 1954 and 1968 the average life of national governments in the Sudan was eleven months.[6] The situation at present remains the same, since the period between May 1986 and June 1988 witnessed three major ministerial reshuffles and three coalition governments.

It is interesting to note that the eras of the two military regimes witnessed relatively more stable governments and that major governmental administrative reforms were initiated and implemented during these periods. In an attempt to increase popular participation and to support local government, General Abboud's government transferred functions from District Commissioners to elected local authorities. At the provincial level, two councils were established: the Province Council, composed of chairmen of local authorities in the province and some elected members, to formulate policy; and a Province Authority, composed of heads of governmental departments (ex-officio members) at the provincial capital, to execute provincial policy. But these reforms were shortlived; in 1964 the military government of General Abboud was forced to resign. It is ironic to note that the democratic parliamentary government which took over ablished the Province Councils, which were to represent the people, and transferred the functions of policy-making, as well as its implementation, to the Province Authority, which was composed of officials only. Thus Province Authorities during the whole era of the second parliamentary government fell into the hands of the bureaucrats.

As we shall see later, Nimeiri's regime advocated and implemented a system of regional government in both southern and northern Sudan. Every region enjoyed an elected legislative body (People's Regional Assembly) and an executive body composed of a Governor and a Regional Government Cabinet. The local government system was also amended to match the few regional governments.

The transitional as well as the parliamentary governments, which took over after the overthrow of Nimeiri, accepted the idea of regional government and accused the previous system of being undemocratic. Thus Regional Assemblies were abolished and their powers were transferred to political Governors, Commissioners, Local Government Inspectors and Officers. That is to say, for the last three years all of the regions, provinces, and local authorities have been run exclusively by bureaucrats.

The Sudan's experience suggests that a democratic, parliamentary regime at the central government level does not necessarily encourage or develop popular participation and representation at the local level; likewise, a military regime at the central government level does not necessarily inhibit or discourage popular participation and representation at the local level. It is worth mentioning that most of the more serious socio-economic planning efforts took place during Nimeiri's regime. Some planners refer to the early years of Nimeiri's regime as the "golden era of planning".[7]

In order to appreciate more fully the role played by the Sudanese bureaucracy in the socio-economic and political development of the country, it is rather important to outline briefly the foundation and present structure of the Sudan's public service. Modeled on the British tradition, the public personnel system is composed of classified permanent, pensionable posts, and unclassified posts. Terms of service of central, regional, and local government's personnel, as well as those of public corporation, are almost similar, though the latter enjoy higher salaries. The public service is divided into three classes: (a) the administrative and professional class; (b) the sub-professional and technical class; and (c) the clerical class. The administrative and professional class accounts for about twenty percent of the public service; it is concerned with the formulation of policy, coordination, general administration, and control of the bureaucracy.

The professional staff are mainly concerned with professional functions, although some of them carry out some administrative duties. Both the administrative and professional class members are recruited from university graduates, with some few exceptions. To these two categories the Sudan looks for the implementation of socio-economic development plans.

Since independence in 1956, the size of the Sudan's bureaucracy, excluding the military, grew from about 23,000 to more than 123,000 in 1975. This represents about 6 percent of the Sudan's population in the same year.[8] By 1983 it had grown to about 300,000,[9] and by 1987 it reached 430,000 government employees,[10]

It has been a common practice for many Sudanese governments to issue directives to governmental departments requiring them to absorb unemployed personnel even if there are no vacancies; for example, during Nimeiri's regime even army officers who were accused of plotting against the regime and as a result expelled from the army were employed by local government under governmental directives.

A quick look at the Sudan's annual budget of 1988-1989 helps us to appreciate more completely the size and influence of the Sudan's bureaucracy.

In June 1988, the Minister of Finance presented to the Constituent Assembly a budget of about L.S. 10 billion (total expected expenditure), with a deficit of about L.S. 4 billion. He argued that the total revenue expected was L.S. 5,969 million, while Chapter One alone, which incorporates the remuneration of the public service (excluding the military), consumes L.S. 1,862, that is more than thirty percent of the total revenue. The military's share of the budget increased from L.S. 850 million to L.S. 1,500 million; thus bringing the percentage of the staff salary costs to more than fifty percent of the revenue.

In order to cut down the number of the public service personnel, the Minister of Finance advocated that the voluntary retirement age should be reduced from 55 years to 45 years and that the compulsory retirement age should be reduced to 55 years instead of 60 years.

As in many less-developed countries, the private sector in the Sudan is weak and small. The government is by far the largest employer; the vast majority of the people outside of government service are either small farmers or nomads; it follows that the lowest paid government employee earns more in cash, enjoys better conditions of service, and generally leads a better life than the average non-government employee. Sudanese local proverbs consider those who get government jobs as luckier and look at the government service as heaven on earth. It is correct, therefore, to note that the line that separates the administration from society is also the one that by and large separates the "educated" from the "non-educated", the "elite" from the "non-elite", and the "better offs" from the majority.[11] The great prestige enjoyed by public servants has probably contributed at least as much as material advantage or employment security to the attractiveness of a bureaucratic career.

Bureaucracy and Political Development

One of the most significant legacies of colonial rule in the Sudan is the importation of Weberian bureaucracy, organized according to Western administrative concepts and incorporating, to some degree, Western notions of efficiency, rationality, and impersonality. As in many less developed countries, the "seed" of bureaucracy found a fertile soil in the Sudan; several other institutions and systems transplanted from the West (e.g. political parties, parliaments, elections) were not as lucky. Bureaucracy grew and proliferated at the expense of the representative institutions, such as political parties and parliaments. The result was a grave developmental imbalance between bureaucracy and those institutions.

Bureaucrats who are aware of their social prestige feel that they are privileged intellectuals. They come to view the bureaucratic institution as the only national one that truly encompasses the whole society and thus is better capable of representing the national interest. This is further enhanced by the short life of the unstable governments, and by the fact that bureaucrats usually have greater security of tenure than party officials, ministers, and members of parliaments.

In less than four decades the Sudanese bureaucracy has had to deal with multifarious and changing political systems. Since independence, it has survived and flourished under multi-party, non-party, single party, parliamentary, and presidential systems. It will be pointed out later that under all of these conditions bureaucracy came out victorious and remained the most dominant institution. None of the representative institutions was capable of controlling or of imposing responsibility upon it. As a matter of fact, bureaucracy assumed many political functions left undone due to the weakness of representative institutions and the absorption and preoccupation of politicians with problems of stability and sheer political survival.

For the purpose of analyzing the role of bureaucracy in the political development of the Sudan, and to avoid repetition, the five political eras stated above will be dealt with under two categories, namely, the parliamentary regimes and the military regimes. The former is characterized by the existence of political parties and elections; the latter incorporates both the non-party system of Abboud and the single-party system of Nimeiri.

The colonial period was predominantly a period of bureaucratic rule. Admittedly, most of the senior political and administrative posts were held by non-Sudanese. Nevertheless, all educated Sudanese, who were mostly post-intermediate school graduates, were employed by the government and hence constituted the indigenous Sudanese bureaucracy. Bureaucrats were seen as forming an elite of talent and wisdom and sometimes they built admirable records of integrity and ability.

It is important to point out that during this period the indigenous Sudanese bureaucracy played a vital role in the political development of the country, in terms of achieving independence, creating political parties, and establishing a parliamentary regime.

Political parties in the Sudan had their origin in the nationalist movement. The Graduate General Congress was formed in 1938 by the post-intermediate school graduates (Sudanese bureaucrats). Although its objectives were ostensibly social and civic, it soon took a political character, making the Congress the focus of the nationalist movement. Four years after its foundation it split into two parts, forming the Umma Party and the Unionist Democratic Party.

During those early days bureaucracy and the emerging political parties were on good terms. The political leaders of the two main parties, the ministers, army officers, and senior government officials of the first self-rule and parliamentary governments were good friends; they went to the same schools and colleges, and worked closely together in the National Congress. Moreover, there was a wide consensus as to the objectives of the early parliamentary governments, namely, Sudanization and independence. As early as February, 1953, a Sudanization Committee was formed "to complete the Sudanization of the Administration, the Police, the Sudan Defence Force and any other government post... within a period not exceeding three years".[12] Sudanization was hurriedly completed. In less than eighteen months, the civil service, the judiciary, the police, and the armed forces were localized. Finally, in 1956, political independence was achieved.

This period also witnessed the end of the honeymoon between the bureaucracy and representative institutions, when national politics, in which all were involved, gave way to party politics.

Political parties soon found support and allies in traditional, tribal, and religious leaders. Almost every party became the mouthpiece of either a religious sect or an ethnic group. Political parties became a reflection of the ethnic, religious, and regional differences in the society. Enlightened bureaucrats felt alienated and withdrew from party politics. Such a situation has continued until the present day.

But the political environment within which the bureaucracy operates, in the Sudan, is essentially pluralist. The inhabitants of the country are racially heterogeneous. The people of the north are primarily Muslims of Arab origin; they constitute about three-quarters of the Sudan's total population. In the south the people are negroid or Nilotic; thus an ethnic boundary existed for centuries between the two cultures. This demonstrates that the whole Sudan is not quite Arabized as some people casually think. The people of the north themselves are far from homogeneous. The northernmost inhabitants of the Nile Valley are Nubians, who have close affinities with the people of upper Egypt; they speak different Nubian languages of Hamitic origin, and Arabic as a second language. The west of the country is occupied by non-Arab Nuba and Fur tribes.

The government is thus confronted with a crisis of identity, the need to develop a unified sense of national unity, to work out an agreeable constitution, and to incorporate culturally diverse elements into the political system. But political parties, in the Sudan, are unable to help in dealing with these crises; on the contrary, they tend to aggravate them.

Unfortunately, political parties, being parochial, are unable to create a sense of nationhood among the varied people of the Sudan. In their present structure, they reflect and add to the sectarian, racial, and geographical heterogeneity of the country. According to the number of seats won in the 1986 elections, five major political parties and blocks can be identified; they are the Umma, the Unionist Democratic Party, the National Islamic Front, the Block of the Southern Regions Parties, and the Western Sudan African Organization, respectively. The Umma Party is supported by the Ansar Sect and draws much of its support from central and western Sudan, while the Unionist Democratic Party is patronized by the Khatmia Sect and finds its support in the northern part of the country. The non-Arabs of western Sudan are organized in the African Front Organization, while most of the small southern parties are united in the Southern Block. And finally, there is the National Islamic Front, which advocates an orthodox Islamic constitution and laws. Clearly, it is a religious party and can hardly claim to represent any non-Muslim Sudanese. It follows that none of the political parties can truly be called a national institution in the sense of embracing all elements in the society, and thus they are ineffective as agents of national integration. Little wonder that the bureaucracy has assumed the integrative function. The bureaucracy feels that it is the only national institution which can claim to represent the whole society.

Party politics is viewed by the majority of the population as corrupt as is also the case with parliamentary and local government elections. Political parties do not hesitate to use corrupt methods—such as buying votes—in their election campaigns. By so doing they bring corruption down to the people and destroy the idea of representation through elections. Moreover, the electoral system itself is alien to the people. The majority of the population are not used to a system of election by symbols and secrets ballots. Is the system they were used to, and before corruption became common, an Omda (tribal leader), who was fairly representative of his people, was elected by the rural people in a special way: "His election is sometimes a lengthy business, being accomplished by means of a process, almost of bargaining—a gradual withdrawal of the less popular candidates until only one candidate is in the field".[13]

Tribalism, sectarianism, and regionalism in party politics and elections favored sons and relatives of the traditional leaders. The educated, urbanized Sudanese bureaucrats could not compete favorably in parliamentary and local government elections. The result was that all parliaments have been dominated by less educated, parochial members of weak calibre. Lofchie correctly points out that in less-developed countries "the influence of administrative cadres is further heightened by a marked discrepancy in technical skills between the bureaucracy and the representative structures, indeed, by the intellectually impoverished character of most party organizations. This gap can easily lead to the complete administrative domination of internal decision-making processes".[14] This is quite true in the Sudan. Political parties, parliaments, and local government legislative bodies are characterized by extreme weakness and fragility. As we shall see later, the situation remained the same under the two military governments. Little wonder then that the bureaucratic sector has gained an overwhelming degree of influence over government policy.

The relative security of tenure of the bureaucracy coupled with the pervasive instability of parliamentary governments have offered the bureaucracy the opportunity of performing political functions otherwise left undone. Political leaders, members of parliaments, and ministers are occupied with the questions of political survival. The actual running of the country is left in bureaucratic hands.

Moreover, bureaucrats, being conscious of their security of tenure, have become more powerful than ministers and politicians. They enjoy long years of service compared with the short political life of the ministers and members of parliaments. The Under Secretary of Local Government, for example, continued in his post from 1954 until he resigned in 1970. He was seen by the public as more important and effective than the minister he was serving under.

It is interesting to note that the first decision taken by the transitional Government's Council of Ministers in 1985 was to consider all public servants who are selected to serve as ministers as officials on secondment; and thus they have the right to go back to their ordinary civil service positions when the term of the Transitional Government is over. For them, ministerial posts, as incentives, are not enough; and the personal consequences of losing their secure civil service positions are extremely serious if not disastrous.

The fact that there is no clear demarcation line between administration and politics gave the bureaucrats the opportunity to narrowly define the jurisdiction of politicians. Socio-economic planning, rural development projects, the organization of self-help schemes and cooperative movements have come to be considered as purely administrative activities. But such activities significantly affect the life of the rural people and hence the social and political relationships in the country.

The apparent adherence to the concept of the political neutrality of public servants and the merit principle as opposed to spoils has greatly enhanced the power of bureaucrats. With regard to the relationship between bureaucracy and representative institutions, Fred Riggs and Lofchie contrast the early Western experiences with those of the less-developed countries. For Riggs, the spoils system, as a method of bureaucratic recruitment, was effective in the development of strong political parties in Western society in the sense that it provided attractive material incentives for party members in terms of occupation of governmental posts. Spoils also made civil service personnel entirely dependent for their positions upon political leadership, and thus encouraged the complete subordination of the administration to the politicans: "Limited spoils recruitment remains an important party activity even today in the United States, but the important point is that by the time merit replaced spoils as the basic method of recruitment, parties had acquired a high degree of functional and organizational autonomy".[15]

But political parties in the Sudan are confronted with an old and well established system of merit recruitment for the public service. This deprives party organizations of important material incentives and stresses the autonomy and independence of the public servant from the politician. Moreover, the concept of political neutrality, which is closely associated with the merit principle, has become the basis for public service resistance to political responsiveness. One of the more recent examples of confrontation between public servants and politicians is reported from the Department of Planning. During his electoral campaign the Minister of Finance and Planning promised his constituents to develop a health centre into a hospital in the Four-Year Plan (1986-1990). But he failed to keep his promise because the Department of Planning rejected the idea and on pure economic feasibility studies allocated the funds elsewhere. The Minister was defeated by his own department. This shows that politicians are not aware that planning is essentially a political process in the sense that its decides priorities in government policy, and hence should not be treated as a purely economic process. Policy priorities and differential resource allocations have become subject to bureaucratic decision. Moreover, it is widely believed that ministers and politicians are often too approachable and liable to accede to requests from the public without adequate grounds, while civil servants, on the other hand, are often too unapproachable and liable to refuse requests without adequate examination and, hence, they are considered to be more objective.

At the local government level, bureaucratic power, during the parliamentary regimes, is seen in the dissolution of the legislative bodies of local authorities and the transference of their functions of policy formulation to civil servants. It is also manifested in the stripping of local authorities of their functions and the entrusting of these to central government departments.

Provincial and local government legislative bodies established by Abboud's regime were abolished. Their functions and powers were transferred to bureaucrats. Likewise, the present parliamentary government dissolved regional and local government legislative bodies established by Nimeiri's regime; their powers are now exercised by bureaucrats, namely: Regional Governors, Commissioners, Local Government Inspectors, and Administrative Officers. Local administration during the three parliamentary eras was then left in bureaucratic hands, without any measure of popular participation. Moreover, the present government on the recommendation of the El Jozali Commission (Prime Minister 1985-1986) decided to reduce the powers and functions of local authorities on the grounds that local authorities were incapable of performing them, and hence recommended the transference of those powers and functions to central government ministries.[16]

It remains to be said that bureaucratic power was not always disfunctional. The two uprisings which led to the overthrow of the two military regimes were led by the bureaucratic sector. In the two events the public service, though fragmented along functional lines, was united in a general strike. The military supported the general strike. Both transitional government's cabinets were formed by a majority of neutral bureaucrats. Those governments were successful in maintaining law and order, in running elections and hence preparing for a smooth takeover by parliamentary governments.

The rest of this section will be devoted to the analysis of the role of the bureaucracy in the political development of the Sudan during the two military regimes, especially that of Nimeiri, 1969-1985.

As in many less-developed countries, the military in the Sudan remains one of the principle forces in the political system. The military possesses the instruments of power and has a cohesive organization. As is the case with the public service, the military feels that it reflects the national interest and has the capability to unify a fragmented society. In recent years there have been many cases, in less-developed countries, of military intervention in domestic politics aimed at restoring order by abolishing unstable civilian regimes. Such intervention has taken place in the Sudan. The literature on the role of the military in the socio-political development of less-developed countries is vast. Some scholars view the military as a conservative force that stands against the introduction of significant changes.[17] Others view the military as champions of change.[18] Bill argues that because it maintains a virtual monopoly on the instruments of force and coercion in less-developed countries, the military is in the best position to carry out either type of program.[19] In his examination of bureaucratic power in less-developed countries, Riggs concludes that the rise to power of military men is in itself a manifestation of excessive bureaucratic power.[20]

In the Sudan, Abboud's regime represents the conservative military. But General Abboud did not seize power by a typical coup d'état. He was rather handed over the government by Abdalla Khalil, the Prime Minister, who was also the Secretary-General of the Umma Party. Mr. Khalil's Government had to face a vote of confidence by the opposition. All evidence has shown that the government was going to lose, and that the opposition would eventually form a new government. When General Abboud was approached by the civilian Prime Minister to take over the government, he hesitated, but after consultation with his senior army officers he took the offer, seized power, banned political parties, abolished the parliament, and formed a military government.[21]

Nimeiri's regime, on the other hand, represents the modernizing military regime. In his first address to the nation, Major General Nimeiri said, ''The revolutionary vanguards in the people's Armed Forces in alliance with other patriotic forces have seized power from the reactionary forces... for the benefit of our people, thereby leading our country into a new era, building its unity, augmenting its economic resources, formulating its social life along the road of socialist development''.[22] It will be pointed out later that, during the two military regimes, preoccupations with administrative reforms mainly centered on decentralization.

In his political and administrative reforms Nimeiri established a single party system, namely, the Sudan Socialist Union (S.S.U.). Instead of the parliament, a People's Assembly was established. Forty percent of its members were directly elected, representing geographical constituencies; ten percent were appointed; and fifty percent were to be elected by the S.S.U. functional organizations (Youth and Women's Associations) and by Trades Unions such as Workers, Farmers, Doctors, Teachers, Civil Servants, etc.[23]

In 1972, a system of democratic regional government was implemented in southern Sudan. A regional parliament was directly elected. It was empowered to elect both its chairman and the Regional Governor. Ten years later, the regional government system, with some amendments, was extended to northern Sudan. A major reorganization of the local government system took place in 1971.

In analyzing the role of the bureaucracy in the political development of the country during the two military regimes, we shall deal first with the relationship between the bureaucracy and the representative institutions at the central level, namely, the S.S.U. and the People's Assembly. Then we shall examine the relationship between the bureaucracy and local government institutions.

The S.S.U., which was a weak political party, was bureaucratically dominated. Frequently, key officals in the regime were appointed, on a ex-officio basis, to commanding positions in the party. Several senior public servants and army officers were appointed as members of the Political Bureau and in the last party reorganization carried out by Nimeiri, four out of six of the commanding positions in the party were filled by an army general, two senior civil servants, and an undersecretary. Even clerical posts in the party organization were filled by civil servants on secondment from central and local government departments.

The party was neither able to monitor the state bureaucracy nor to direct it. It was too weak to constrain bureaucratic power. The public was hardly able to feel the existence of the S.S.U.; Nimeiri and his assistants frequently accused the party of being ineffective; yet it was needed to legitimize and rubber-stamp some of the regime's policies.

Bureaucratic power flourished even more during Nimeiri's regime. Ministers were mostly selected from the bureaucratic sector. In Nimeiri's frequent reshuffles many undersecretaries were appointed ministers in their departments and for many of them, ministerial posts became normal promotions. A cursory look at the membership of Nimeiri's cabinets reveals that bureaucrats were in the majority. For example, in the 1981 Cabinet, the writer has calculated that out of a total membership of 33 ministers, 21 were ex-civil servants and three were army generals.

Neither the party nor the council of ministers was important during Nimeiri's regime. The country was run by the President and the bureaucrats. In a public speech in November, 1981, Nimeiri declared that he had abolished the political party and dismissed all ministers and their deputies. Next day he left Khartoum for Washington; for about four weeks the country was run exclusively by bureaucrats. Nimeiri's frequent reshuffles were demoralizing to the ministers and led to discontinuity in the political leadership of governmental organizations. An observer described Nimeiri's rapid reshuffles and his practice of constant movement of persons from one position to another as "a chessway of playing with posts." Civil servants who were more secure and stable assumed the functions of political leadership. In turn, this added to the power and strength of the bureaucracy.

In contrast to the situation during the parliamentary regimes, the bureaucrats during Nimeiri's military regime dominated the People's Assembly. The electoral system permitted public servants to nominate themselves and contest the Assembly's elections without resigning from their posts. Many public servants stood for the elections and won; moreover, there was a considerable number of seats in the Assembly reserved for the representatives of the bureaucratic sector, such as army officers, doctors, university staff members, administrative oficers, teachers, agriculturalists, veterinarians, engineers, etc. As expected, there were tremendous educational and social gaps between the ordinary Assembly member, who was much less educated, and the bureaucrat as a member. Bureaucrats became the beginning and end of the People's Assembly. Ordinary members were led by bureaucrats. The People's Assembly became a defender of bureaucratic rights; it was no longer an extra-bureaucratic power to control the bureaucracy. In a famous case during the term of the Fourth People's Assembly, the Assembly declined to back up a Presidential decree empowering ministers to dismiss public servants on the grounds of lack of political responsiveness. It was the only incident in which a presidential decree failed during Nimeiri's regime.[24]

It remains to be said that in spite of the weakness of the various People's Assembly and their inability to control the bureaucracy, none of them was able to run its full life. The Second, the Third, and the Fourth People's Assemblies were dissolved by Nimeiri before the completion of their terms of office. The Fifth People's Assembly's life was terminated by the April uprising.

As pointed our earlier, during the two military regimes decentralization represented an important theme in government reorganization. As early as 1960 General Abboud established Province Councils and Province Authorities. The former, which were legislative bodies, were composed of elected members and chairmen of local authorities and some ex-officio members. Province Authorities, on the other hand, were composed of governmental department heads at the provincial level. They were entrusted with the executive functions.

In an attempt to increase the participation of councillors, Nimeiri introduced a new system of local administration, which was set down in the Local Government Act of 1971. At its simplest, the Act introduced a pyramidal structure at the local level. At the apex was the People's Province Executive Council (P.P.E.C.) which, in a sense, was an amalgamation of the two provincial councils of 1960. In that comprehensive system of local government, all services to the citizen were to be provided by the P.P.E.C. through its subordinate councils; hence several functions were transferred from central government departments to the P.P.E.C. Representatives of central ministries were ex-officio members of the councils and shared responsibility for both decision-making and implementation. The idea was to break down the dichotomy between bureaucrats and councilors and to commit the former to the policy they were supposed to carry out.[25] Although the Act specified that the number of ex-officio members should not be more than one third of the total membership of the council, their influence was much greater. They were all-powerful. The ordinary councilor seldom had the courage to question, let alone stand against, suggestions and decisions made by the bureaucrats. This was partly due to the low capability of ordinary councilors and partly due to the historically high status of bureaucrats. In this respect, the Union of Local Government Administrative Officers argued that opportunities for involving councilors in policy formulation and executive actions were limited; and that the effort involved in doing so was greater than the importance of the issue; and that unnecessary delay would be the result.[26] Partnership between bureaucrats and councilors in making and implementing the council's resolutions failed. Bureaucrats were in full control of local authorities.

The system of bureaucrats sitting with councilors as members was done away with by the introduction of regional government in northern Sudan. In 1981, regional legislative bodies were elected. They were empowered to pass regional laws and supervise the administration of the regions. The Regional Governors were responsible to both the Regional Assembly and the President. The local government system was also reorganized to match the new regional government system. Local authorities' legislative bodies were elected; they were empowered to pass local orders and supervise the administration of the local councils. Executive functions were entrusted to administrative officers.[27] But these reforms, which were intended to reduce the bureaucratic domination over local government representative institutions, were shortlived. Three years later Nimeiri was forced out of office and eventually the bureaucratic sector regained its supremacy over all other sectors.

Bureaucratic power at the local level reached its climax after the overthrow of Nimeiri's regime. Regional and local legislative bodies were abolished and their functions were transferred to bureaucrats. Regional and local government elections are not among the priorities of the present parliamentary government. The same state of affairs existing during the parliamentary government which succeeded the Abboud regime. Province Councils were abolished and their functions were transferred to bureaucrats. During the whole era of that parliamentary government no Provincial Councils' elections took place. It is ironic to note that the military regimes were keener on participation and local democracy than the parliamentary governments. Popular representative bodies, during the parliamentary regimes, stopped at the central government level; they were extended to neither regional nor local government levels. Moreover, during both military and parliamentary regimes, power remained in the hands of the bureaucratic sector; political parties, parliaments, and local government institutions were weak and fragile and were bureaucratically dominated.

Bureaucracy and Socio-Economic Development

As pointed out earlier, the bureaucratic sector is directly engaged in the translation of policies into action and in the formulation and implementation of socio-economic plans. Success or failure in the attainment of goals is logically attributed to it. But the record of the Sudan in socio-economic development is one of recurrent failures. The country which has been called the "food basket of the Middle East and Africa," because of its ability to feed a large number of countries, is not yet self-sufficient in many agricultural commodities; and it is still subject to the vagaries of drought and famine. To feed its people the Sudan imported in 1958 about sixty thousand metric tons of corn. In less than three decades the amount of imported corn rose to over sixty million metric tons; that is to say, one thousand times as much.[28] In 1981 the bill for imported food commodities was about L.S. 150 million; by 1985 it had grown to over L.S:. 250 million.

Nowhere in the Middle East or Africa does the paradox of "wealthy but poor" manifest itself as it does in the Sudan. The country is endowed with vast land and various water resources as well as favorable soil and suitable climatic conditions for developing agricultural production. Out of a total area of approximately 600 million feddans, about 200 million feddans are at present suitable for agricultural production; and out of this about 17 million feddans only are currently under cultivation, i.e., less than ten percent of the total arable land.[29] Despite the under-utilization of its agricultural potential, the Sudan is heavily dependent on agriculture, which accounts for about forty percent of its Gross Domestic Product (G.D.P.). The share of the agricultural sector in the total labour force amounts to more than eighty percent.[30] But agriculture in the Sudan has not yet received attention corresponding to its importance.

As far as economic development is concerned, the Sudan is classified among the twenty-five least developed countries. The G.D.P. per capita in 1968-1969 was only $113 compared to the African average of $105 and the Arab countries' $252.[31]

Since its independence the Sudan has been faced with problems of slow economic growth, worsening balance of payments, deteriorating terms of trade, slow-growing exports, and mounting debts. In the words of a Sudanese economist, "by 1981 Sudan graduated from the stage of an economy in 'crisis' to an economy in a 'deepened crisis' ".[32]

In analyzing the role of the bureaucracy in the socio-economic development of the Sudan, we shall examine the changing patterns of planing policies and the problems of implementation. It will be argued that there is a wide gap between plans and their implementation; unrealistic plans have unduly raised the hopes and expectations of the people. It will also be argued that poor implementation of socio-economic plans is attributed to bureaucratic in-fighting, fragmentation, and lack of coordination; but implementation often requires collaborative efforts among the varied governmental departments. The Management of the National Economic Conference in 1987 commented that, "there has been a notably rapid deterioration in the performance of the public service and an obvious failure on its part to assume its responsibilities. The bulk of the state machinery has failed to direct the state's economic and financial activities or to promote their performance. As a matter of fact the very organs charged with the duty of promoting the state's financial resources have, in fact, become a burden on the Exchequer".[33]

Planning in the Sudan has had a chequered history, with ups and downs corresponding to political changes taking place in the country. The status and authority of the planning organization have also undergone extreme changes since independence.

As early as 1951, a small planning unit was established in the Department of Finance and Economics. The first separate development plan was published in 1951-1952 and since then expenditure on development has been allocated a separate budget. However, until 1960 only annual development budgets concerned with expansion in educational and health services were prepared. Shortly afterwards General Abboud's government, being anxious to launch more ambitious programs of socio-economic development, boosted up planning.[34] As early as 1961 an Economic Council, a National Technical Planning Committee, and an Economic Planning Secretariat were created. The Economic Council was chaired by General Abboud; its members included the Prime Minister and some senior Cabinet Ministers. The Development Committee was itself a Ministerial Committee; it was empowered to submit recommendations to the Economic Council on the development plan after considering the recommendations of the National Technical Committee. The latter, which was charged with technical coordination and follow-up of the plan, was assisted by the Economic Planning Secretariat.

Accordingly, a comprehensive Ten-Year Development Plan (1961/62-1970/71) was drawn up. It was expected to generate an annual average growth rate of 5.2 percent in the G.D.P. However, the Ten-Year Plan did not run its full life, because in 1964 the October Uprising marked the end of the Abboud regime.

The early days of the second military government witnessed a new era of centralized comprehensive planning. Nimeiri's government, which was anxious to give shape to its socialist program of socio-economic development, created a full-fledged Ministry of Planning. Socio-economic planning was given a prominent place in the governmental machinery. A team of Russian experts was attached to the new ministry. The Russian team soon produced the first Five-Year Plan (1970/71-1974/75). This aimed at an average annual growth rate of 7.6 percent in the G.D.P. However, the life of central comprehensive planning was also short. In 1971, the Sudanese Communist Party was accused of plotting a coup against Nimeiri's regime. Its leaders were tried and some of them were executed. The Russian planning team was dismissed and their Sudanese assistants lost their positions. The planning organization had its share in the ordeal; it was downgraded from a full-fledged Ministry to a department under the Ministry of Finance. The Five-Year Plan lost its force and appeal, leading to deterioration in the achievement of goals.

Soon afterwards Nimeiri's regime started to consider seriously the possibilities of attracting Arab money to the Sudan. It was believed that many of the Arab countries equate the strengthening of public-sector dominated planning with greater control over the private sector. Concern about attracting Arab money was reflected in the Six-Year Plan (1977/78-1982/83). The Six-Year Plan, like its predecessor, aimed at an average annual growth rate of 7.5 percent in the G.D.P. As far as foreign financing was concerned, the plan assured the existence of guaranteed external sources as the result of agreements with various Arab countries.[35]

The rest of this section will be devoted to the examination of some of the problems of implementing the plans.

It has been pointed out earlier that bureaucracy, in the Sudan, is overweight. It consumes over fifty percent of the total annual revenue. Nevertheless, the increase in size of the public service did not lead to many qualitative changes in the administration needed for better implementation. The implementation performance record of all the plans has been rather poor with administrative inadequacies being among the major constraints. Some scholars summarized such problems of implementation as being the inadequacy of the planning machinery, the lack of trained manpower, the inadequate preparation of project reports, delays in construction, problems of liquidity, and delays in external and internal purchases of machinery and equipment.[36]

As early as 1972 the Ministry of Planning, complaining about poor follow-up, commented that, "It is to be noted with concern that many of the ministries and departments do not submit, as required, the underlying reasons and obstacles inhibiting the effective execution of their respective projects".[37] In a recent study, a Sudanese economist enumerated seven major industrial projects which were supposed to be productive between 1977 and 1981 but were still lagging behind in 1986.[38]

The National Planning Commission attributed this slow realization to "transport bottlenecks, liquidity problems, slow and unsatisfactory utilization of loans, red tapism and the incompatability between desk planning, execution and follow-up capabilities of some key government units".[39] A close observer of the industrial scene noted that there had been undue haste in setting up factories, without proper studies of availability of suitable raw materials and marketing possibilities.[40]

Several examples of such mistakes can be sited. The sugar project of El Guneid was not properly located. The Agriculture Research Division had this to say about the site: "North Central Sudan is not the correct place for growing sugar cane... and best yields cannot be expected." A Sudanese expert pointed out that the "soil was already exhausted due to successive cotton cultivation... that the studies were carried out by a party which did not like to spend more time and money to seek other alternatives... other questions still remain unanswered about the preparation of the technical requirements, staff training etc. before actual construction has taken place. Everything seems to have been forced in an unplanned way".[41]

Another example came from the Babanousa milk drying factory. The factory was not able to utilize more than twenty percent of its capacity due to non-availability of milk in the area. The inhabitants of the area were nomads who did not stay in the area for more than two months each year. The factory is now drying "Karkadei," a local soft drink. The stories of the Kassala onion dehydration factory and the Karima fruit and vegetable canning factory are also similar. When the former started production, it was discovered that there was little market for dried onion flakes in Sudan, where fresh onions were available throughout the year. The latter suffered from problems of transportation. The Aroma cardboard factory faced similar problems and had to be closed down.[42]

A former undersecretary, (A. Mirghani), of the Planning Department gives many illuminating examples of how several development projects were delayed and costs increased due to inadequate understanding of administrative processes. In one case of terminating a contract for construction, because of an inordinate delay in the issuance of a notification, the Government lost an arbitration in the dispute and had to pay the consultants over L.S. 60,000 in claims and had to secure the services of another consultant at a cost of over L.S. 200,000, while the sum remaining to pay the previous consultant to fully complete the work was not more than L.S. 50,000. In the second case, the contractors proved to be incompetent and were bankrupt. The contract provided for a notice before termination of services; but their services were terminated without such notice with the result that instead of losing their deposit and being liable for claims for any extra cost of completing the work, the contractors won an arbitration award of one million dollars. In the third case, the Government had to pay compensation of a quarter of a million to a contractor as his work was delayed due to the Government's inability to acquire the site of the bridge in time. But "the avoidance of disputes in carrying out construction projects in development plans is an essential matter. Contract disputes are expensive... [and] reputable firms may not tender under such circumstances, or if they do, may inflate prices". Mirghani correctly concludes that the "personnel concerned with the implementation of projects ought to be properly trained as administrators and business managers. This is especially necessary in the case of technical people who often deal with big constructional projects. In many countries such technical people, especially engineers, think that knowledge of administration and business management is given to them by heaven. It is not"...[43] but it ought to be learned.

Lack of coordination, bureaucratic in-fighting, and professional jealousies are among the more serious developmental obstacles.

The importance of agriculture and animal resources in the Sudan cannot be over-emphasized. Development of integrated crops and animal programs suffered as a result of fragmentation of this work within a number of ministries and departments; paramount among them were the Ministry of Agriculture and the Ministry of Animal Resources. The former included the Departments of Agriculture, Forests and Land Use, and Rural Water Development. The latter included the departments of Game, Fisheries, and Husbandry. Each department produced a separate plan. The Agricultural Development Conference of 1964 observed that "agricultural development in Sudan has no boss".

In 1964, the Director of Agriculture wrote a letter to the Director of Husbandry suggesting the formation of a working party from the two departments to explore the possibilities of cropping and stocking systems and to consider the possibilities of integrated agriculture-animal husbandry. This initiative for cooperation was met by an angry reaction. It is revealing and interesting to quote, at some length, the reply of the Director of Husbandry: "The working party which you propose to set up or which you already formed should be purely the concern of your own department as long as its terms of reference are confined to crop production. But if the party will consider matters pertaining to Animal Husbandry as you say, then this Ministry should have been brought well into the picture, because it is the Government Agency for the development of Animal Husbandry in the country, a fact which cannot be ignored. Therefore your request just to nominate a part time cooperator is not palatable.

We have suffered a lot in this country from imported ideas which in many cases do not fit into our local conditions and which in most cases may be taken for granted like a message from Heaven. Your Proposed Working Party will only add a little extra to the complication. Crop husbandry in this country still has a long way to go and you have too big a responsibility to develop your crop husbandry without complicating the issue by trying to carry the heavier load of animal husbandry. The country still suffers from a lack or shortage of many foods; wheat, rice, sugar, tinned vegetables, fruits, coffee, tea, etc., etc., are still imported and in my opinion you will do a great service to this country if you augment your efforts to make this country self-sufficient in these products rather than try a shift into animal production. You know that there is no lack or shortage of animal proteins in this country to justify your intervention or that of an Advisory Body".[44]

The contents of the letter reveal only too well the coordination problem in the agricultural sector. The various departments dealing with agricultural development were so conscious of their departmental independence that they were not willing to recognize the interdependence of their responsibilities.

In 1973, on the advice of many experts and international organizations, the various departments dealing with agriculture, food, and natural resources were forcefully brought together under a new Ministry of Agriculture and Animal Resources. But bureaucratic in-fighting and professional jealousies between veterinarians and agriculturalists continued to prevail. In 1985, under the pressure of the Veterinarian Association, the Ministry was once more split into two separate ministries. The vicious circle has started again. Such are the problems of socio-economic development in the Sudan.

Conclusion

In the Sudan the bureaucratic sector is dominant and all-powerful. There is a grave developmental imbalance between it on the one hand, and parliaments and political parties, as representative institutions, on the other. Bureaucracy has restricted the growth and development of such representative institutions; it has assumed many political functions and thus hampered political development.

Being powerful as it is, the bureaucratic sector has not succeeded in achieving a tangible level of socio-economic development; thus, there is an ever-widening gap between the rising expectations of the people and the real achievements. Administrative inadequacies, lack of coordination, and bureaucratic in-fighting are among the more serious obstacles to socio-economic development.

NOTES

1   El Rashidi, F. Human Aspects of Development; International Institute of Administrative Sciences; Brussels, 1971, (p. 5).
2   Waldo, W. Toward World "Development"; African Administrative Studies; Cafrad No. 16; (1976) (p. 93).
3   Lofchie, M. F. Representative Government, Bureaucracy, and Political Development: The African Case; African Administrative Studies; Cafrad No. 16; (1976) (p. 129).
4   Moharir, V. V., and Kagwe, S. Administrative Reforms and Development Planning in the Sudan; (1956-1970), Development Studies and Research Centre; University of Khartoum, 1987, (pp. 10-11).
5   Massanat, G. S. The Dynamics of Modernization and Social Change: A Reader; Goodyear Publishing Company, Inc. Pacific Palisades, California, 1973, (pp. 207-208).
6   Abu Sin, A Major Administrative Reforms in the Sudan; a paper prepared for the Inter-Regional Seminar on Major Administrative Reforms In Developing Countries, Falmer Brighton, U.K., 25 October-2 November 1971, (p. 8).
7   Moharir and Kagwe. *Ibid.*, (p. 26).
8   Ministry of Public Service and Administrative Reform; Sudan Government, 1976, (p. 7).
9   Awad M. H. Arabian Contemporary Administrative (In Arabic). Arab Journal of Administrative. Vol. 9 No. 4; Fall 1985, (p. 7).
10 Management of The National Economy Conference, Khartoum, 28-31 January 1987, Development and Research Centre, University of Khartoum, 1987.
11 Doornbos, M. R. Bureaucracy and Development: Where Are The Constraints? African Administrative Studies; Cafrad No. 16; 1976, (p. 19).
12 Sudan Government; Self Determination; 1956, (p. 12).
13 Marshall, A. H. Report On Local Government In the Sudan; Khartoum, 1948, (p. 41).
14 Lofchie, M. F. *Op. Cit.*, (p. 134).
15 *Ibid.*, (p. 133).
16 El Jozoli, D. "Report on Local Government In the Sudan" (In Arabic) Sudan Government, 1987, (p. 19).
17 Shills, E. "The Military in the Political Development of the New States. In John, J. J. *The Role of the Military in Underdeveloped Countries*, Princetown Press, 1963, (p. 31).
18 Halpern, M. *The Politics of Social Change in the Middle East and North Africa*, Princetown Press, 1963, (p. 253).
19 Bill, J. A. "The Military and Modernization in the Middle East"; in Masannat, G. S. (ed), *The Dynamics of Modernization and Social Change*, 1973, (p. 448).

20   Riggs, F. "Introductory Concepts"; African Administrative Studies; Cafrad No. 16; 1976, (p. 90).
21   Beshir, M. O. "History of the Nationalist Movement in Sudan (1900-1969) (In Arabic) Khartoum, Sudan, 1987, (p. 229).
22   Sudan Government Preamble; Khartoum Press, 1969, (p. 2).
23   Sudan Government; Elections Committee; People's Assembly Election's Regulations, (In Arabic) 1982, (pp. 2-6).
24   Sudan Government; Records of the Fourth People's Assembly; (In Arabic) Omdurman, 1980.
25   Alassam, M. "Decentralisation in the Sudan"; Ministry of Information, 1979.
26   Union of Local Government Officers, Khartoum, 1975.
27   Al Assam, M. "Regional Government in the Sudan", *Public Administration and Development*, 1983, Vol. 3.
28   Macro Economic Policies Conference; Khartoum, 13-15, January 1986; Development Studies and Research Centre, Khartoum University.
29   Sudan Government; The Five Year Plan; Khartoum, (p. 40).
30   Ali, A. "Some Aspects of the Sudan Economy"; Development Studies and Research Centre, Khartoum, November 1984. (p. 9).
31   Moharir and Kagwe, *Op. Cit.,* (p. 10).
32   Ali A., *Op. Cit.*, (p. 27).
33   Management of the National Economy, *Op. Cit.* (p. 1).
34   Moharir and Kagwe, *Op. Cit.*, (p. 28).
35   Nimeri, S. An Evaluation of the Six Year Development Plan in the Sudan (1977/78-1982/83); Middle East Studies and Research Centre, University of Khartoum, 1978, (p. 51).
36   Moharir and Kagwe, *Op. Cit.*.
37   Sudan Government, Ministry of Planning Economic Survey, 1973, (p. 93).
38   Salih, A. M. "Financial Policies in the Sudan" (In Arabic) Macro Economic Policies Conference, 1986, (p. 177).
39   Economic Survey, *Op. Cit.*, (p. 113).
40   Ali, A. H. "Inadequacies of Industrial Services in the Sudan"; Mimeographed, October, 1973, (p. 31).
41   *Ibid.*, (p. 32).
42   *Ibid.*, (pp. 5-6).
43   Mirghani, A "Development Planning in the Sudan in the Sixties"; Graduate College Publications, Monograph 2, University of Khartoum, 1983, (pp. 178-180).
44   *Ibid.*, (pp. 175-176).

Bureaucracy and Development in Saudi Arabia: The Case of Local Administration

IBRAHIM AL-AWAJI

Ministry of the Interior, Kingdom of Saudi Arabia

ABSTRACT

This paper examines the role of the Saudi bureaucracy in development by focussing on local administration. It points to several shortcomings of the Saudi local administrative system, including diverse organizational structures, low educations qualifications of local public officials, imbalance between the executive authority and the assigned responsibilities of local agencies, a high degree of duplication, and lack of co-ordination of services. All of these constitute serious obstacles to the Saudi local administration playing an effective role in promoting socio-economic and political development. Despite these shortcomings, however, the Saudi local administrative system has been active in the dynamic development of the Saudi Kingdom. This active role has been strengthened by national development plans which emphasize the development of the Kingdom's geographic regions through the establishment of regional development centres.

THE HISTORICAL AND GEOGRAPHICAL status of Saudi Arabia on the one hand, and the modern development that accompanied the petro-economic uprise on the other, have brought forth a unique and rich experience worthy of research and study not only for the sake of recognizing its positive outcome, but also in order to examine the obstacles and adverse situations in the way of this experience which I hope will contribute, as lessons, to the enrichment of research and practice in our Arab societies with a view to developing their administrative institutions according to the Arabs' own criteria.

However, in order to identify the distinguishing features of Saudi local administration, it is important to review its development as well as its functional role. It is my assumption that the reader is aware of the basic facts about Saudi Arabia. The space limitation imposed on this paper has compelled me to limit my coverage of many important elements and much of the background of the subject.

A. Background of the local administrative system

The most important aspect in the very foundation of the new state of Saudi Arabia contributed by its founder, King Abdul Aziz, was the concentration of his efforts in completing the political build-up of the country. Its geographical unification, the keeping of order, and the preservation of the consolidated territorial *status quo* without interfering in the local systems of the regions of the Kingdom, were, King Abdul Aziz's priorities rather than the unification of administrative systems.

It is a well-known fact that the Kingdom was composed of quite different areas as regards population conditions, local circumstances, and contacts with adjacent frontier areas. The vast area of the country, the communication difficulties, and the fact that the central authority was mainly concerned with security affairs, were all logical factors that retarded the attempt to consider any radical change in the then existing structure of local administration in the Kingdom. This may account for the relatively advanced administrative system in the Western province at the early stages of the national foundation, a fact which is attributed to the presence of the Islamic holy places there, where the pilgrimage and seasonal visit activities brought the area into constant contact with the outside world, producing the subsequent social effects. Further to this, the region was, shortly before that time, under Turkish domination. Therefore, its administrative system was, at this stage, adopted as the basis for the central management which grew up gradually thereafter.

In view of the above, the local administration can be divided into two categories. The first is the one which was followed in the central, eastern, and southern provinces, where the local agencies, being very conservative, have stuck to their traditional patterns which means that their main activities were focused on juridical and financial fields. The second category[1] was organizationally a sounder system as the administrative activities in the Western province involved municipal, health, and other services besides juridical, financial, and security services.

The following is a review of the then existing administration organizations.

a. *National and Municipal Councils*

At the top was the National Council (or Board) established by King Abdul Aziz in 1343H composed of 15 members in addition to the chairman.[2] This council supervised all government agencies. Its functions and responsibilities were as follows:
1. Arranging municipal affairs and drawing up internal systems of regulations for the municipality to guide it in the performance of its duties;
2. Keeping control over the courts to see that justice was duly observed;
3. Reviewing endowment affairs and payments;
4. Preserving internal security and arranging for the required police forces;
5. Taking care of education, particularly religious education;
6. Facilitating commercial activities and promoting the post and telegraph services; and,
7. Establishing permanent national committees to solve internal day-to-day problems according to social traditions and Sharia.[3]

A town committee was established composed of 14 members from amongst the citizens of Jeddah to oversee the progress of internal town affairs. Then the Constitutional body was formed, partly elected and partly appointed, representing all towns of the province.[4] This was later followed by advisory councils established in Mecca, Madina, Jeddah, Yanbu, and Taif to handle local affairs. In 1345H the basic Regulations for Rule and Administration were decreed.

Being mainly concerned with local administration in this paper, I deem it relevant to mention that orders have been passed to establish the following local agencies:
a) Consultation Council (Shoora) in Mecca[5];
b) Administration Councils in Jeddah and Medina;
c) Township Councils; and,
d) Rural and Tribal Affairs Councils.

Each of these councils will be composed of members drawn from key officials and eminent persons of the town, township, village, or tribe.[6]

b. *Governors' and Administrative Councils' Regulation*[7]

This regulation was issued on 13/1/1359H in two parts to define the functions, duties, and powers of governors not only with regard to the maintenance of security and justice, but also with respect to their supervision of government agencies in their respective districts.

The second part dealt with administrative councils. An administrative council composed of four to eight elected members was established in every gubernatorial jurisdiction. The function of these councils was to look after all affairs of the area such as adherence to the official regulations and instructions; the investigation of complaints of citizens against government workers; the supervision of tenders, contracts, wages, and approvals thereof; the development of local projects; the handling of the affairs of foreign visitors; government purchases; the issue of licences for construction or other projects in the area; etc. These councils still exist throughout the Kingdom.[9] In 1359H Cabinet Resolution No. 545 was issued to specify those cases in which a public worker might hold membership in these councils.

With the development of the central government agencies and their local branches, the importance of these councils diminished so greatly that their role in many cases was restricted to the selection of tribal leaders and their deputies. This situation also applies to the Municipal Councils which shrank to a level of minimal importance with the rise of the new municipalities that receive orders from the central authority (the Ministry of the Interior and later the Ministry of Municipal and Rural Affairs).

c. *Local Services*

The existing services pursuant to the instructions issued on 21/2/1345H, in addition to the regular agencies such as Justice, Security, Foreign, Military, and Financial Affairs, were:[9]

the Directorate for Health;
the Directorate of Post and Telegraph;
Municipalities; and,
the Directorate of Public Education.

This indicates that the local services at the stage of formation of the state were limited and more or less concentrated in the areas where they originally existed. With the improvement of the financial situation and human development, these local services started gradually to expand horizontally to cover more and more districts and regions of the country while other services in various fields were successfully established.

From this historical review of the local services at the stage of the state build-up, it is clear that local administration was characterized by the following:

1. Incompatibility of the local agencies in the various provinces, towns, and villages with respect to their organizational set-up and service quality stemming from historical, organizational, and financial reasons. All these, in fact, demonstrate the difficulties through which the country was passing at the stage of national foundation.

2. Administration in the Kingdom first started from the local administration in the Western Province and expanded horizontally and vertically to become the nucleus of public administration in the Kingdom. Therefore, administration was deeply affected by the local administrative traditions and values of the Western Province.

3. The administrative systems adopted in the first decade following the founding of the country were characterized by decentralization and participation in local affairs. This is due to a lack of structural elements in the main Managerial Agencies, which were only young organizations at the time. This fact also accounts for the trend toward centralization which accompanied the expansion of the central government agencies and their dimensional growth. In the early phases of administrative development, the system was too centralized and had hindered local activities. This, however, cannot be attributed to an intended governmental policy of keeping a strong hold on power as much as to the standard of the then prevalent administrative mentality and decision. Yet, such an attitude may be vindicated, for it is not a lack of confidence in local officials but the shortage in the local administrative leadership that is to blame.

B. The New Era

Although eight Ministries along with several independent key agencies were established prior to the establishment of the Council of Ministers as a central administrative authority in 1373H, the setting up of the Council is considered a crucial starting point in the establishment of the modern administration system in the Kingdom. Nevertheless, this does not in practice mean the occurrence of an abrupt radical change of management in the provinces and towns and in their relations with the central agencies. Services started to spread more widely after the development of the oil industry, i.e., after the Second World War. The rate of progression of these services was also normal until 1376H when the ministries moved to Riyadh and started to take up their assignments. One of the healthy organizational features was the tendency to consolidate or separate service organizations with a view to facilitating a more efficient discharge of their duties in the fields of municipal works, electricity, water, communication, and toad services. This is an important development that has reflected the quantitative and qualitative expansion of services and the need for improving these organizations and agencies so that they can better shoulder their responsibilities.

These developments were a direct incentive for the Government to issue the Provincial Regulation in the year 1383H as an expression of the desire to encourage local management. This regulation gave the provinces considerable authority in local affairs, particularly in public services. In line with this, provincial governors enjoyed vast powers to approve and decide action on local affairs. This regulation was later reconsidered in order to bring it up-to-date to suit the new, extensive development plans and programs in the period being reviewed in this study, i.e., the past thirty years.

Anyone who traces the organizational development of the Ministry of the Interior can clearly recognize the serious trend towards a uniform provincial administrative organization. Supporting evidence for this tendency is the fact that many small governorships such as Beisha, Yanbu, Afif, and Khasera, which were previously connected directly to the Ministry of the Interior, exactly as the major provinces of Riyadh, Mecca, and the Eastern Province, now became connected to the main districts within whose jurisdictions they were located. So, the end result was that the Kingdom was divided into fourteen provinces with independent budgets under the control of a governor at the rank of Minister having broad executive powers over local affairs.

Among other signs of this trend was the establishment of the Ministry of Municipal and Rural Affairs in 1395H entirely as a local service organization. In addition, the issuance of the Regulation of Municipalities and Villages in 1397H stating that a municipality is a legal entity with financial and administrative independence is also a further positive stand in favour of the tendency to encourage local participation. However, from a very narrow and yet a favourable outlook, this can be seen as a sort of return to the organizational roots prevalent at the early stage of a state's formation.

Six types of local organizations of various degrees of authority and with different geographical range come under control of the Ministry of Municipal and Rural Affairs in the Kingdom of Saudi Arabia. These are follows:

1. *Municipalities*

There are five municipalities in the cities of Riyadh, Jeddah, Mecca, Madina, and Dammam and a major municipality in Taif. They possess a wide range of authority over local municipal affairs, such as town planning and design, construction projects, housing affairs, etc. Several local municipalities are associated with each of these, since they are located in their jurisdictions, including township and townquarter municipalities.

2. *Directorates General for Municipal and Rural Affairs*

There are eleven directorates throughout the Kingdom supervising nearly 90 municipalities and 53 rural village groups. These directorates are connected directly to the Ministry of Municipal and Rural Affairs, as is the case with the six major municipalities. The Directors possess vast authority in the area of local municipal and rural affairs, but somewhat less than the authority delegated to the Mayors of the large cities.

3. *Rural Groups*

The Ministry of Municipal and Rural Affairs, with a view to extending needed services to more than ten thousand villages scattered throughout the Kingdom, where it is practically impossible to handle their affairs and needs through the existing municipalities, has established 53 rural headquarters to extend services to villages, particularly to those showing aptitude for growth and stability. These organizations act under the Rural Development Plan issued by a Cabinet Resolution in 1402H (1982). They manage all municipal activities at the level of each group of villages.

4. *Water and Sewer Departments*

The radical changes that occurred in the urban environment in the Kingdom within the last two decades were simultaneously accompanied by the need to provide these modernized towns with up-to-date and sufficient water supplies and sanitary drainage systems. Therefore, the Government has established, by a Cabinet Resolution, five separate water departments concerned with the planning and execution of the local main systems and local distribution networks. They were given semi-independent authorities. Each department is under the control of a Board of Directors, chaired by the respective Provincial Governors and including the membership of the Deputy Ministers of the Ministries concerned, such as the Ministries of Finance, Agriculture, Health, and Municipalities, together with the respective city Mayors, along with other members appointed by a Resolution of the Minister of Municipal and Rural Affairs, who is responsible for the supervision of these Departments.

5. *Higher Committee for Town Development*

In response to the need for coordintion of the different governmental non-municipal servies in the cities and for the setting up of a higher joint command with vast authority over development, the Council of Ministers issued Cabinet Resolution No. 717 in 1974 for the formation of the Higher Committee for the development of Riyadh city under the presidency of the Riyadh Governor and with the membership of the Mayor and the concerned deputy Ministries. It was given authority to approve major policies and to carry out the city development plan, as well as to provide coordination between governmental agencies and private sectors in the field of development. Toward this end, a special agency was created mainly for the purpose of coordination, preparation, and follow-up to carry out its responsibilities in connection and in coordination with the municipality. An executive committee which is directly connected to the Higher Committee for Town Development was also created for the New Diplomatic Quarter together with a special technical office concerned with development of the Old City. Other higher committees were set up in the other principal cities, but they did not have the same role and effectiveness for many reasons, one of which was the appearance of disagreements regarding decisions and actions to be taken. This resulted in interference with the responsibilities and tasks of the municipality and the other governmental agencies and especially the Ministry of Municipal and Rural Affairs. The question of applying the experiment in general is still the subject of argument and research.

6. *Other Local Organizations*

In the field of the other services such as health, electricity, communication, agriculture, and water, etc., the last two decades have witnessed a major development in the establishing of provincial departments or branches to supervise services and to represent the Ministries and the other central agencies in the capital, although these departments and branches differed considerably as regards their organizational levels and responsiblities from one Ministry to another and from city to city according to the different prospects of the region or the city.

This is what makes the issuance of a standard regulation or the setting up of a uniform organizational system an imperative necessity. However, the shortly anticipated issuance and implementation of the Provincial Regulation may provide the remedial action for this organizational defect.

The new local administration is characterized by the following main variations:

C. Important Characteristics of Modern Local Administration

As already hinted above, the Ministries and independent administrative organizations follow different systems of division of their branches in provinces or cities ranging from the level of Directorate, Department, Branch, etc., thus leading to remarkable dissimilarities in level and number between these divisions of the various ministries. A true picture of the situation may be seen in the fact that the Kingdom is now divided into fourteen provinces which are supposed to be the appropriate organizational settings for the ministerial branches in these areas. But the reality is quite different since, for example, the Ministry of Health has eight branches while the Ministry of Agriculture has fifteen branches, whereas the Post and Telephone departments, on the other hand, have different geographical divisions. What has been said about the numerical variation may also be said about administrative levels, as some ministries are represented in these provinces by directorates or departments while others are represented only by provincial headquarters or branches. There is also a problematic geographical distribution of services as every Ministry has its own geographical method of placement of services, although they deliver similar services to their respective recipient areas.

A more critical aspect of this organizational interlacement is that branches of some ministries in some towns or Emirates are connected to bigger branches within the jurisdiction of another Emirate or province. The town of Umloj, for instance is connected administratively to Tabouk Emirate while its Health, Agricultural, Educational, and Postal Affairs are connected to Medina, and it reports to Makkah in regard to Juridical and Communication Affairs. While the town of Tima itself is connected to Tabouk area, Health Affairs, Justice, and Girls' Education are connected to Medina whereas Boys' School Affairs are linked to Tabouk and the local religious/moral authority is connected to Hail. The Municipalities of the Northern Border and Al-Qurayyat are connected to Al-Jouf. Road and Health affairs of Jizan and Najran are linked to the Asir district.

This situation is due to several factors, some of which stem from the historical or traditional background of the department or organization. It may have stuck to its old organizational structure without the kind of change which occurred in the entire governmental machine or the ministry to which the department or oganization belongs. Another reason may be that the ministries do not look at the new administrative division of the country into fourteen provinces uniformly in view of the lack of a standard organizational system to be followed by all government departments. And a further reason may be the shortage in administrative possibilities (mainly manpower) and the subsequently inability to set up complete provincial departments.

One of the common characteristics of the local agencies is the low level of the educational qualifications and the incompetence of the employees due to the poor incentives offered them compared with those in the cities. This is a phenomenon which accompanied the change in the standard of living and the rapid development in the other cities, a fact which raises the rate of movement of qualified nationals from the local agency to jobs in the minor cities.

In general the local agencies have the problem of a lack of balance between their executive authorities and the responsibilities assigned to them. However, this differs from one governmental sector to another, depending on the leading personalities, the nature of the activities, and the relationship between the leading administrators in the ministries and the responsible officials in the branches. But usually decisions are taken by the central agencies where key officials do not have the proper level of understanding of local needs.

Although the regulation for provincial governors and administrative committees, mentioned above, provides that the local agencies shall be subject to the direct supervision of the governor of the region, yet the reality is the opposite of this. If we exclude some cases in which the governor exercises a general supervision over the government agencies which is more or less a sort of personal initiative and differs in its effect from one department to another, we note that the general trend is toward the independence of the local agencies and the tendency to report to their respective central administrations in the capitals to which they belong. This has resulted in much duplication and lack of coordination of services. It is a problem that will hopefully be resolved by the issuance of the new Provincial Regulation.

Conclusion

The task of the local agency is no longer that of the previous traditional symbol or representative of the central authority or, at its best, a local agency offering limited services in its field of specialization. It is now that of an active agency in the dynamic development which the country is going through. If the economic situation and the administrative organization to go farther than its limits as a service provider, today the role assigned to the local agencies is totally different as regards their developmental implications as well as the nature and size of their activities. The reason for this is that the activities of a local agency in a given place are connected and correlated with other local agencies where the social and economic development plan is being implemented. This is what the third and fourth five-year plans have demonstrated. One of their principal goals is the development of regions through what are called development centers in the Kingdom. This national responsibility which is assigned to the local agencies by the central authority in addition to their original responsibility of representing the interest of the people of the region, city or village, puts the local administration in a new position as an important agency to achieve the goals of government and of the public, to improve the standard of services, and to properly represent them as an efficient intermediary between center and base.

For these reasons, it is imperative to take prompt organizational steps that will assist with the new responsibilities placed on the local administration. Such steps as the following might well be undertaken:

1. The speeding up of the issuance of the Provincial Regulation in its new form so as to provide an important organizational framework in the field of coordination among the various governmental agencies, thus minimizing duplication effects, as well as the amount of national participation in the decisions that concern each province.
2. The issuance of a standard governmental administrative organization for the local administration in the Kingdom providing for administrative authorities of equal rank.

Models of High Achievement in Local Administration

Since the middle of the last decade, the cities and towns of the Kingdom have gone through a record crises due to the economic boom experienced by the country, the huge developmental plans, and the extensive internal migration from rural areas to towns, where the boom-related work opportunities and financial interest were highly inviting. Government plans included new kinds of service projects such as water supply systems, electricity, road construction, landscaping, modern municipal residential plans, and housing loans for citizens, etc.

Municipal services were previously being offered within the limits of the financial and administrative situation prior to this stage through an administrative organization suitable to the level of the then existing services. The local agencies, and the central agencies as well, were to plan and execute urban development within an inconveniently short period of time that was quite inappropriate to the available manpower and organizational capabilities. This has created a real administrative crisis which in turn gave rise to acute competition among the administrative organizations in the country and between cities and villages. The criteria for administrative efficiency and adequacy became:

1. The ability to control the new situation, including its financial, technical, and administrative responsibilities; and,
2. The ability to benefit from the development circumstances and the generous projects which the country has planned to achieve the highest possible degree of urban modernization.

The problem was of two dimensions. The first concerned the standard of knowledge and ambitions of the local leaders in modernizing their regions, and the second concerned the administrative situation as regards (1) efficiency of employees, (2) adequacy of the information system, (3) the official and administrative procedures which started to change radically at the beginning of the first stage at the central administration level, and (4) dealing with the other equal-ranking agencies of ministries and regional administration and breaking through the authorities and the communicational barriers which themselves were undergoing a similar stage of entanglement. The opportunity was available for talented local and central administrative leaders to achieve progress within the existing rules.

This, in fact, occurred in more than one city and village. Among these achievements a significant and distinguished qualitative accomplishment emerged in the city of Jeddah on the coast of the Red Sea and in Hail in the north within the same general circumstances prevalent in other towns and locations considering the fact that all districts are subject to the central and regional agencies and the same public administrative and financial regulations though the status of each of the two examples differed one from the other. Jeddah is the second largest city in the Kingdom after Riyadh and had enjoyed a traditional commercial status as a leading trade center compared with other towns. Further, it was the center for Diplomatic Missions at that time and it is the sea entrance to the Holy Makkah. Therefore, the idea of developing Jeddah received special political attention and the personal support of His Majesty the King himself. On the other hand, Hail is a desert town which before this stage of developmental enjoyed the same care and attention given to other similar towns.

The role played by the local administrative leadership represented the most important factor of distinction in the ability not only to derive optimal benefit from the available financial possibilities, but also to adopt innovative methods in comparison with what was going on in the other towns during the same period of time when the change was taking place. So, the two experiences became examples that other municipalities endeavored to follow. They were models of action that directly contradict the efforts of the others. The two experiences became the topic of public opinion and media discussion. Jeddah, in its new and attractive look, with its picturesque coastal scenery and wonderful corniche, as well as its beautiful public gardens, is called "The Bride of the Red Sea." Hail, on the other hand, is now as "The Bride of the North," in view of its natural desert beauty coupled with its new urban planning and fine gardens. This developmental success is not restricted only to the change in the appearance of the two cities, but has involved the creation of a local social atmosphere they can well be proud of in view of the sense of positive participation of their citizens, i.e., the most important accomplishment was the creation of a collective consciousness and a common sense of responsibility among citizens, thus moving them from the state of indifference which results from the misconception that the government is responsible for everything. Everyone may recall, for instance, how some people in Jeddah used to pick out the marble tiles from the public garden pavements, but soon thereafter turned to protect and preserve such facilities and to respond sincerely to all procedures regarding improvement of their city; they even offered financial contributions when required.

These accomplishments took place under two innovative local leaderships with no common educational or professional background binding the two men together. The Mayor of Jeddah was an ambitious architect, namely, Mohammad Saeed Al-Faresi, who started his career as an engineer in Jeddah municipality. But his gifted sense of leadership and artistic imagination, impelled by a great love for his hometown, enabled him to leap quickly to the top where he rushed forward into serious action to translate his ambitions into unique projects and works utilizing all available means and breaking through the routine and procedural restrictions in an intelligent compromise between his aspirations and these restrictions.

The Mayor of Hail, on the other hand, was an administrator and academic specialist in Islamic Sharia and Arabic Language. Though he had not received particular training in public administration or local management, yet his high intelligence, talent, and aggressiveness were his fighting tools against the then existing routine and other administrative barriers in the way of realizing his ambitions. He followed a plan of work based on two points, the development of the administrative and executive Municipal Organization and optimum employment of financial allocations beyond the rules and instructions usually followed in practice and in accordance with the development programs as viewed by him. He was thus able to accomplish appreciable achievements within notably limited financial means, a job that could never be accomplished under any other administrative leadership.

However, although these two cities share some characteristics, they differ in many others. The educational and personal backgrounds of the two Mayors were different; so were their experiences, historical, and financial backgrounds. But each of them has carried out his own ideas following his own methods and approaches. The mutual factor was their natural ability to do distinguished work, their enthusiasm, courage, and ability to use the existing resources and circumstances. Both of them achieved and used some unfamiliar methods. However, Jeddah has her own taste and characteristics while Hail has different but equally remarkable ones.

NOTES

1   Al-Awaji, Ibrahim. *Bureaucracy and Society in Saudi Arabia*, Ph.D. dissertation, University of Virginia, U.S.A., 1971, Pages 43-45.
2   *Um-al-Qura Gazette*, issue (3) dated 29/5/1343H, and *Um-al-Qura Gazette*, issue (32) dated 16/1/1344H.
3   *Um-al-Qura Gazette*, issue (32).
4   *Um-al-Qura Gazette*, issue (52) dated 11/6/1344H.
5   *Um-al-Qura Gazette*, issue (71) dated 2/11/1344H.
6   *Um-al-Qura Gazette*, issue (90) dated 25/2/1345H, and issue (91) dated 3/3/1345H.
7   On 7/1/1375H a Royal Order was decreed for dissolution of this council. On 9/1/1346H the Regulation for this council was issued to be followed by an amended new regulation one year after.
8   For further details regarding assignments and formation of Councils refer to the basic instructions published in *Um-al-Qura Gazette*, issue (91) dated 25/2/1345H.
9   Refer to *Um-al-Qura* issue (133) dated 1/1/1346H and issue (134) dated 8/1/1346H.

REFERENCES

AL AWAJI, Ibrahim
     1983   *Development of Local Administration in Saudi Arabia.* Municipalities, UAE, February. (in Arabic)
AL AWAJI, Ibrahim
     1971   *Bureaucracy and the Society in Saudi Arabia*, Dissertation for Ph.D., University of Virginia, U.S.A.
ABDUL MU'TI, Assaf
     1982   *Principles of Local Administration & its Application in Saudi Arabia*, Al Fahoom Co., Amman, Jordan.
ABDUL MU'TI, Assaf
     1983   *Administrative Organization in Saudi Arabia*, Dar Al Oloom, Riyadh. (in Arabic)
ABDUL RAZAK, Mohammad Nuraddin
          Principles of Administrative Science, (Applied Study in Saudi Arabia), Al Khadamat Bookshop, Jeddah, Saudi Arabia. (in Arabic)

AL BLEIHI, Ibrahim
    Hail District and Municipal Services, 1981, Hail Saudi Arabia. (in Arabic)
ALJAHANI, Eid Mas'ud
    1984 *The Council of Ministers in Saudi Arabia between Islamic Sharia & Contemporary Constitu-
        tional Trends*, Riyadh Publication House, Riyadh. (in Arabic)
AL MOHANNA, Mohammad Saleh
    1983 *Finance of Local Administration and its Application in Saudi Arabia*, Institute of Public
        Administration, Riyadh, Saudi Arabia.

Bureaucracy and Development in Egypt Today

NAZIH N. AYUBI

University of Exeter, Exeter, U.K.

ABSTRACT

In spite of the adoption of an open door economic policy, the size of the Egyptian bureaucracy continues to grow, and its control functions remain quite significant. There is very little retrenchment in the economic role of the bureaucracy, although that role is now much less integrated with any comprehensive plans for national development. The main preference seems to be for a joint venture formula between the public sector and foreign capital. The most important casuality of this practice has been the Egyptian public sector itself.

Since THE OPEN DOOR economic policy was formally adopted in the mid-seventies, the role of the Egyptian public bureaucracy has undergone several changes. Such changes, however, do not amount to a "retrenchment of the State", as some observers have interpreted them. The state bureaucracy is still large and expanding, both in terms of personnel and expenditure, and the control functions assumed by the bureaucracy have by no means declined. In the economic sphere, the public sector has not really given way to the private sector (except in the special case of commerce and finance), but the State has merely chosen to cooperate with international capital. This has signified a transformation of the state's role from a developmental one to a production-oriented one (seeking profit and cutting down on welfare activities *within* the joint public sector/international capital enterprises). However, the welfare functions of the state bureaucracy toward the society at large (education and health, food subsidies, etc.) have not been significantly curtailed, although the state has become increasingly dependent on external sources for financing them. The purpose of this article is to review some of these developments, using the public sector as a main focus of analysis.

Bureaucratic Growth

Contrary to many expectations, the Egyptian bureaucracy has not slowed down its expansion, in terms of personnel or expenditure, as a result of adopting the Open Door Policy (*infitah*) in 1974. Public employment continues its phenomenal growth: in 1986/87 the state employed some five million people out of a labour force of some 13 million (of which about 500,000 were in the armed forces and about two million were working abroad).[1] This means that at least 40%, and most likely more, of the civilian labour force, resident in the country, work for the state.[2] Of these, 3.4 million were in the civil service (roughly evenly divided between central and local government) and 1.6 million were in the public sector, just under half of them engaged in industry. Bureaucratic expenses also remain very high. Out of a total public expenditure of some £E20 billion in the 1986/87 budget, £E3.865 million was earmarked for wages and salaries, and £E8.670 million was allocated for other current expenditures (including £E1.746 million for subsidies). This compares with £E7.467 million earmarked for investments and £E2.317 million for capital transfers (payment of domestic and external debts, financing deficits, etc.).[3]

Itemized figures are available for the period 1977 to 1980/81, and their analysis reveals some very interesting characteristics of the bureaucratic growth that has taken place.

Public Personnel

Bureaucratic personnel grew noticeably even *after* the adoption of infitah. In only three years from 1977 to 1980/81, employment in the bureaucratic machine increased from 1,911,000 to 2,474,000 i.e., by 29.6% or some 10% per annum. This is about four times the population growth rate during that period (2.6%) and actually surpasses the rate of bureaucratic growth even at the highest stage of "socialist transformation" in the sixties, when it reached about 8.5% annually.[4]

Bureaucratic growth did not take place, however, in an even way across all sectors. In spite of the rhetoric about decentralisation and local government, employment in the central bureaucracy increased during the same period by 60.4% whereas it increased only by 28.7% in local government.[5] Within these general figures, specific employment in public welfare services grew by only 5.4% and in public economic organisations by only 4.1%. This reveals that the "conventional" rather than the "developmental" bureaucracy has received the main bulk of the new recruits. The growth in public personnel also tended to be proportionately larger at the top echelons of each category of the bureaucracy: thus ministerial posts (to include governors) grew by 48.4%, undersecretaries by 130.1%, and directors-general by 126.1%. However, higher posts in general increased by 25.9%. In the remaining categories, although middle management positions had increased by 155.7%, the lower executive and administrative posts had grown by only 114.5%.[6]

Looking at the expansion by sector we find that it was unfavourable to several "developmental" sectors. With the exception of the industry and petroleum sector, where personnel grew by 145.2% (partly due to the expansion in the petroleum industry following the "oil boom"), the largest expansion between 1977 and 1980/81 took place in law and order sectors (defence, police, and justice) by 212.6%;[7] in insurance by 162.1%; in supplies and commerce by 142.1%; and in the Presidential (Sovereignty) services by 140.3%. The lowest growth rates were in electricity and energy, 63.4%; in culture and information, 67.8%; in tourism and aviation 113.1%; in agriculture and irrigation, 116.0%; and in education, research, and youth by 120.8%. Thus, in general, we notice that growth in personnel has been on the whole more favourable to law and order, "sovereignty" and other control and "repressive" organs of the state bureaucracy than it has been to the "developmental" and social welfare sectors (with the exception of oil and some industries).

Public Expenditure

Public expenditure in general did not decline either, as a result of the adoption of the open door policy. If anything, the percentage of total public expenditure to GDP had grown from 48.7% in 1976 to 62.9% in 1981/82 (at current prices). This indicates that the economic role of the State bureaucracy had actually grown under infitah, especially with regard to income distribution.

Total public consumption had indeed grown in the four years following infitah (1976 to 1980/81) from £E3.2 billion to £E5.9 billion (i.e., by 84%). Not all of the increase was due to expansion in developmental activity, but was caused rather by the huge growth of the "law and order" and repressive organs of the State (e.g. Central Security Forces, State Security Investigation, State Security Courts, and the so-called "Morals Courts", the armed forces, etc.).

Expenditures on law and order grew from £E91.5 million in 1976 to £E241 million in 1980/81 (i.e., by 263.% at current prices, and by 139.6% at fixed prices). Their share of total public consumption increased from 3.6% in 1976 to 4.1% in 1980/81. Expenditure on the armed forces increased by 152% during the same period although its share of total public expenditure had decreased from 22.6% in 1976 to 18.2% in 1980/81. This remained a high percentage and military expenditure was, in any case, soon to resume its upwards climb.

By contrast, expenditure on education remained unchanged and its share of total public consumption stayed almost the same: 10.9% in 1976, and 11.0% in 1980/81. Expenditure on public health decreased, however: its index number in fixed prices dropping from 340 in 1976 (1962/63 = 100) to 273 in 1980/81, while its share of total public consumption remained the same in 1980/81 as it had been in 1976 (i.e., 2.9% of the total).

The general conclusion applicable to both 1976 and 1980/81 is that expenditure on law and order was in both years about double the expenditure on education and health (26.2% : 12.9% in 1976, and 22.2% : 12.9% in 1980/81). The political and developmental implications of this are significant, as the first type of expenditure represents the "repressive" function of the State, whereas the second represents its role in reproducing the labour force and improving its productivity.[8]

We can thus conclude that, the open door policy notwithstanding, the Egyptian bureaucracy has continued to expand in terms of personnel and expenditure. This expansion, however, has been more remarkable in areas related to the "control" or repressive functions of the State than it has been in areas related to its "service" or socio-economic functions. The figures surveyed above confirm that the role of the state bureaucracy has by no means declined, although it has witnessed some important changes, a proposition that I have argued in detail elsewhere.[9] In the following pages we further suggest that, unwilling to relinquish its control functions, the bureaucracy has had to adjust its economic role from that of a "developer" to that of a "producer" and a "trader". To understand this shift, we need to examine briefly the nature of the crisis that, from the late sixties, started to beleaguer the Egyptian State.

Étatism vs. Populism: The Egyptian State in Crisis

Nasserist Egypt was both "étatist" and "populist". The regime had tried to manage both growth and welfare, production and distribution, or in the jargon of that era, "sufficiency and justice". The contradiction between these two strands in the make-up of the Egyptian state reached its peak after the end of the first five-year plan (1960-65), and the adoption of a second plan was not possible, due to the decline in domestic and foreign financial resources, and then—more dramatically—to the aftermath of the June 1967 war.[10]

As with most other populist regimes relying economically on a policy of import substitution and politically on the state bureaucracy, the Nasserist regime had come to face a crisis in the late sixties, a crisis that was not only caused in this case by the technical limitations of the import-substitution strategy, but that was aggravated politically by the 1967 war and its aftermath. The Nasserist state was reluctant in demanding immediate social sacrifices from the major social classes in order to continue with the regime's developmental projects.[11] The state bourgeoisie then split into two wings: one in favour of private capital and economic liberalism; the other in favour of strengthening state capitalism and maintaining public controls.

The Sadat leadership came to favour the first wing, and the main thrust of the open door policy was indeed characterised by an apparent retrenchment of the economic role of the state and an opening up to private capital—foreign and domestic—as well as a political rapprochement with the West. Yet that policy orientation has not produced in the Egyptian case outcomes similar to those that it produced in other cases (such as Brazil and Argentina) where it did help with the promotion of industrialisation, although at the high cost of rising social tension. What is it then that distinguishes the Egyptian case from some of the other experiments in liberalisation and privatisation?

Infitah: a **State** Policy

In spite of some confusing signals at the beginning, it is now our view that the adoption of the open door policy was in the main an attempt by the State bourgeoisie to adjust its étatist policies to the changing domestic, regional, and international conditions, with a view to preserving étatism and not to jettisoning it. If the Sadat regime (1970-1981) was in any sense manifesting the signs of a "soft State", this was not actually taking place in the sense that the State's control function was being relinquished, but rather in the sense of its failure or disinclination to extract surplus for the purposes of capital formation and development.[12]

It is our contention that infitah has been a master policy developed by the Egyptian state to preserve itself, and especially its étatist role in the economy and the society, within changing political and economic circumstances. This does not imply that the movement towards infitah was always easy, clear, and void of contradictions, but we believe that the outcome enables one sufficiently to build up an image of what has been happening, and to detect in it the very "visible hand" of the State.

From the start, the main ideological movement calling for infitah in the late sixties and early seventies came from *within* the state establishment, with its political leadership and its public sector, and not in any significant way from the domestic capitalist sector. Indeed the main beneficiary so far from the open door policy, especially in the industrial field, has been the government establishment, which has been able through that policy transformation to preserve its main hold on the economy and to continue with its tight control functions. By contrast, the domestic industrial private sector has never had a known history of calling for economic liberalism, nor has it in any significant way benefited from the application of infitah; indeed, some say that this sector has become rather unfavourable to infitah, which strengthened the link between the state sector and foreign capital, leaving the domestic private sector more or less "outside the game".[13]

There is no significant relinquishing of the leading economic role of the State, then, but rather a transformation in the nature of that role. Egyptian state capitalism is gradually reducing its links with domestic capitalism and deepening its links with international capitalism, and the Egyptian State is increasingly playing the role of the intermediary between foreign investors and the domestic market.

In the period following 1977 (the year in which extensive food riots occurred), it had become increasingly clear how limited the role of infitah was going to be in creating a real capitalist transformation that would be led by private domestic capital. The state now began to resort to new methods for tightening its grip on the society and redirecting its economic path, but in a way that would not entirely dissuade foreign investments. At this juncture it became apparent that the ruling elite did not sympathise with domestic capital (in fact the earlier ideas of "selling" the private sector to national investors were never carried out as we shall see), there was an almost total break with Arab capital (with Camp David and the separate peace with Israel 1977-79), and the State opted instead for direct cooperation between the industrial public sector and international capital.

The open door policy thus developed under the impact of the State bourgeoisie opting for alliance with international capital, more than it did under any pressure from the local industrial capitalists. This means that the Egyptian state bourgeoisie has simply chosen new ways to continue to dominate the state and to benefit from its economic resources.[14] This transformation was achieved through various conflicts in the State arena—at the political levels, among various ministries and public sector leaders, in the media, trade unions, etc.—and "Bureaucratic Politics" represented a major process of achieving this transformation, which was mainly realised through the state machine and with the presence of the military and security apparatus as a final guarantor for the regime.

The outcome of these developments is a picture that still contains vagueness, contradictions, and question marks but which is nevertheless capable of some comprehension. It is a picture of a State that cannot continue with both a developmental function and a welfare function at the same time, but that hosts an entrenched State bourgeoisie that is keen on preserving its distinction in power and wealth. This State is thus confronted by a dilemma which it tries to solve through disentangling the previous ideological and political link that existed between its developmental and its welfare functions, by encouraging the public sector units to work for profit (even if it means that public industrial corporations will have to involve themselves in commerce), and by removing from the public companies their welfare functions (concerning wages, pensions, security of tenure, workers' representation, etc.). When these public companies appear to reach their maximum capacity in terms of productivity and profitability, the State then stretches out its hand to international capitalism to seek its cooperation with the Egyptian public sector in "joint ventures".

This leaves domestic capital with available opportunities for investment only in the commercial and financial sectors (reinforcing its so-called "parasitic" character), while a small domestic industrial capital is desperately trying to acquire the same advantages offered to foreign capital/public sector joint ventures. The main trend within the State bourgeoisie has indeed looked at domestic private capitalism with disdain, thus pushing it further into the area of commerce and finance, where it has entrenched itself and has become prepared to defend its interests against the State with great vociferousness.

From a "Developmentalist" to a Profit-Making Function

The development of the infitah policy represents, therefore, in reality an improvisation on the étatist theme, not a victory for the domestic private sector over the State.[15] The adjustment has not been as difficult as it could have been, because although the State has reduced the welfare functions of public enterprises, it did not have to cut back abruptly and completely on the welfare functions at the level of the society at large, which it inherited from the populist mantle of the Nasserist era (e.g. education, health, food subsidies, etc.). This was made possible by the availability to the State at that juncture of significant financial assets, accruing mainly from foreign sources (tourism, the Suez Canal and SUMED, and oil, as well as foreign aid).

As the maintenance of a certain minimum of the State's welfare function is necessary for the survival of the regime, the State has chosen to sacrifice its developmental role rather than its welfare function. Infitah has basically meant a disentanglement of the welfare function of the State from its industrialisation function: Étatist policies are continued in the area of subsidies, the provision of employment, and basic services, whereas in the area of industrialisation, the State becomes merely a large investor among other investors, striving like the others for profit, and cooperating with international capital if this is perceived as the best way to realise profit. The State's role in the economy has thus shifted from an overall developmental role to a producer's role; i.e. from a role where industrialisation forms a major pillar in a general policy of comprehensive national development to one where the State is one among several industrial investors seeking profit, even though it remains the largest among these investors.

It is curious that most investments under infitah (a policy that aimed to encourage foreign capital) in fact represent Egyptian and not foreign projects, and that the main share in the capital of *industrial* projects is, more specifically, Egyptian state capital. Of all infitah projects up to the end of 1981, two-thirds of the total capital was Egyptian (divided roughly equally between the Egyptian public and private sectors), and we notice in particular that state investment was concentrated in the field of industry and especially in metallic works (where the State was almost the sole investor), in addition to a sizeable investment in the area of "contracting".[16] The State's new role as a capitalist investor interested in profit rather than socio-economic development is illustrated by the fact that 44% of the capital of infitah banks was owned by the State—for these are the very banks that invest most of their foreign currencies abroad rather than use them for the financing of industrial development within Egypt!

The main impact of infitah in practice has been distinctly "commercial". The search for profit has become the "name of the game", even for the public sector. Several industrial public companies have had to resort to some trading activities to remain financially afloat and to escape the fate of abolition. And it is symbolically significant, to quote one example, that the Company for Selling Egyptian Manufactures (public sector) which was originally established as part of Tal'at Harb's efforts in the twenties and thirties to promote Egyptian industry, now trades mainly in imported, non-Egyptian products in order to stand up to the financial requirements of the infitah era.

The State bureaucracy in general is also following a "commercial" attitude towards the citizen in offering commodities and services. Thus, for example, there are "special" speedy deliveries of durables, houses, etc., if one pays in foreign currency. Previously standardised subsidised goods and services are now sold in various categories under various prices; thus in food there are ordinary, improved, and de luxe types of bread, and ordinary, improved, and "touristic" grades of rice; and in public transport, there are ordinary, special, and de luxe categories, etc. There are also special prices for faster governmental services: so that one pays higher fees for obtaining a "fast" telephone, or a "fast" passport, as distinct from waiting in the usual queues and paying the normal rates!

The Bureaucracy and Foreign Capital

But why has not foreign capital rushed into investment in Egypt, given the various facilities and privileges offered under the policy of infitah, and what is the role played by the State in this respect?

There are various causes for the lack of foreign investment: the political instability of the region as well as Egypt's separation from the rest of the Arab World after the peace treaty with Israel is one reason. But there is also the notorious Egyptian bureaucracy with its ponderous weight and its slow, rigid, and complicated procedures. It is possible that, in order to sustain itself and to prove that its services cannot be dispensed with even in the infitah era, the Egyptian bureaucracy has been trying to safeguard its survival through a contrived stimulation of "demand" over its services, especially in the area of licences and permits, and by creating all kinds of complications that only the bureaucrats can solve.[17] In addition, infitah created opportunities for making "good" use of public office for private accumulation. Thus in some ways the bureaucrats have no interest in making things easier for the investor; on the contrary, the more difficult the better, as the official can then extract the price for facilitating matters when the "terms" are right. Infitah has, as well, built up its own bureaucracy, especially in the fields of trade, customs, currency, and fees.

Then among the reasons for the reluctance of foreign capital there is the additional fact that the regime was not solid and strong enough to be able completely to dismantle the State's inherited welfare functions and to float the Egyptian labour force as individual workers in a "free" labour market, controlled and disciplined by the State in the Korean mould. There was considerable resistance from within the public sector itself to its being dismantled and sold to private investors, and to floating its labour force and nuclearising it. International capital was not prepared to take too many risks with what it regarded as still a "spoilt" labour force.

On the other hand, the mainstream within the government and the bureaucratic elite was in favour of the public sector cooperating with foreign capital in the form of direct joint ventures. Some saw in this a way of rescuing the public sector from its financial and production crisis, others saw in it an opportunity to improve their own careers and investment prospects. In fact, the public industrial sector was so keen on alliance with foreign capital that it often sold its own assets to the foreign partner in return for using the latter's commercial brand name (as happened between the Ideal Refrigerator Company and Thompson's Corporation); or it joined with foreign capital to form companies that actually competed with the existing public companies in marketing the same products (such as in the case of the Public Company for Batteries, Al-Nasr Company for Rubber Products and Tyres, the Public Company for Electric Products and Transformers, and the Public Company for Elevators and Air Conditioning).

For its part, international capital has welcomed the cooperation with the public sector, which enjoys a dominant position over organisational and human resources in the country and which still possesses a number of monopolistic and preferential advantages within the economy, as well as a number of important political and administrative capabilities. Partnership with the State sector is on the whole a safer bet for international capital in Egypt's current circumstances. Furthermore, foreign investors wanted to benefit from the significant foreign aid that came to Egypt from foreign and international agencies after Camp David, and which accrued directly to the State. Indeed the USAID and the World Bank have sometimes required, as a condition of offering credit to public sector companies, that they should enter into joint ventures with the private sector, both foreign and domestic.[18]

To summarise this section, one can say that a contradiction has grown within the contemporary Egyptian State between two strands in its makeup: a developmental strand that includes, but is not confined to, its étatist or producer's role, and a populist strand that includes the welfare functions of the State. The State was unable or unwilling to solve this contradiction through reliance on the social and economic resources of the society, and decided instead on an externally-oriented and two-handed solution—the one being to relinquish much of the State's developmental role and to confine itself to a producer's role in conjunction with foreign capital, and the other being concurrently to seek an increase of the foreign and ''rentier'' type resources available to the State in order to continue to offer the minimum amount of ''welfare'' services that could not be withdrawn for social- and political-security considerations. To complement this last option individuals were also encouraged to seek foreign resources for themselves (mainly through working abroad) in the hope that this would encourage ever larger segments of the society to reduce their reliance on the State.

Bureaucratic Politics

Within the bureaucracy itself, ''bureaucratic politics'' remain as important as ever, although again manifesting themselves sometimes in different ways. In the Nasserist era, the setting-up of parallel agencies charged with similar tasks, the existence of overlapping jurisdictions among various organisations, and the practice of frequent, sudden appointments and dismissals, were all used to enhance the power of the political leader. The result was continuous competition for turf, for the leader's approval, and for resource allocations.[19] The charismatic leadership and the political ''core'' were so powerful, however, that it is arguable that much (although definitely not all) of the rivalry was manipulated in the direction of developmental efforts.

Following infitah, the competition continued, but the political "core" was weaker, and the leadership was unable or unwilling to manipulate the inter-organisational fighting towards specifically developmental objectives. In addition, a great deal of the competition is now over linkage points with the private sector—both personal links (i.e. for the managers themselves) and institutional links (i.e. for the public organisation at large)—and also over access to external finance (from foreign or international aid-donors and investors).[20] A public manager investing privately in activities very closely related to those of his public office illustrates what is now quite a familiar pattern. Public companies sub-contracting to the private sector or borrowing from the so-called "Islamic companies" are also a usual pattern today. The availability of foreign and international grants and loans has had far-reaching influences as well. Within the resource-hungry bureaucracy, access to outside resources has the potential not only to make a certain enterprise, administration, or governorate "richer" than its competitors at the same organisational level, but sometimes even richer than the "parent organisation" itself. This gives rise to intra-organisational as well as inter-organisational rivalries. With USAID and the World Bank (among others) currently favouring decentralisation and agriculture in Egypt, several examples of such intra-organisational rivalries (and imbalances) can be observed in the local government and agrarian sectors.

Given the traditional weakness of the Ministry of Planning and the current resistance to its influence by certain powerful ministries that have access to external funding (such as the Ministry of Agriculture and the Ministry of Industry), it is reasonable to assume that development policies and projects are currently not being thoroughly coordinated within the bureaucratic machine. Furthermore, the armed forces have, in the eighties, become seriously competitive with the civilian public organisations in the field of development; their activities now extend to many and various spheres, which range from building and construction to production and industry, and which include in particular the so-called "food security" projects.

Indeed, one can imagine certain areas where policies might be better coordinated with elements outside the bureaucracy than they would be with elements within it. Several bureaucrats may now be more amenable to the influence of private capital and foreign investors than to the influence of fellow officials elsewhere in the bureaucracy. New interest groups are emerging to represent and defend the evolving constellation of interests within the country. Particularly influential is the Association of Egyptian Entrepreneurs (*Jam'iyyat rijal al-a'mal al-misriyyin*), where the interests of segments of the state bourgeoisie, domestic investors, and international capital coincide. In addition to ex-ministers and officials, the Association includes a large number of members of the Boards of banks and of public sector companies (in industry and trade), as well as private import-export "big shots" and commercial agents (28% of all members in 1984) and investors in the fields of foodstuffs, textiles, furniture and, of course, tourism, and consultancy. Foreign capital is represented through contributions from ''affiliate committees'' (e.g. the Egyptian-American Committee of Businessmen) and from a number of inter-national finance agencies.[21]

Impact on the Public Sector

The impact of all these transformations on Egypt's struggling public sector has on the whole been quite damaging. It is our view that, all things con-sidered, many of the public sector industries have not been doing badly in relative terms; the decline that many of these enterprises are going through at present is in fact in large measure a result of the application of infitah.[22]

Up to the declaration of the open door policy in 1974, the public sector was responsible for 77% of all industrial production in the country, for 72.6% of petroleum and its products, 78% of construction works, 100% of electricity production, 76.8% of transport and communication, 50.9% of trade, 100% of finance, and 78.8% of services. It contributed 54.5% of total GDP, generated 85.9% of total national savings, and undertook 90% of all national investments.[23] This public sector included some 380 economic units (corpora-tions, companies, etc., each possessing various factories, shops, or branches) of which 239 units were in production, 75 units were in finance and trade, and 66 units were in services.

In terms of managerial personnel, the economic public sector was being run by 34,000 managers (from Board Chairmen down to Class Four executives) distributed among the various public authorities, organisations, and companies. The majority of these managers, about 20 thousand or 57.7%, were university graduates (including hundreds with higher degrees). In terms of career paths, 31% of the public sector managers had started their careers in pre-nationalisation private companies, whereas the others had come to economic management through governmental, academic, or military career lines, and many had, in fact, learned of the availability of their posts through ''personal contacts'' (43%) or through other channels not directly related to the activities of these economic units.[24] It could, of course, be argued that the percentage of managers with no background experience in business was very high, but one should remember that the native private sector was extremely small (and part of it extremely hostile to the 1952 Revolution), and that the ambitious and speedy industrialisation programs of the Revolution had required an accelerated expansion in the public sector.

The adoption of the open door policy has led to an end to public control over the ''commanding heights'' of the economy, by allowing private capital into the areas of finance, heavy industry, and foreign trade. It also abolished the ''public organisations'' (mu'assasat 'amma) as general ''holding corpora-tions'' of planning and coordination, and allowed the various public sector units extensive managerial liberties but deprived them of the privileged position they had previously enjoyed in receiving finance from State banks. As the principle of comprehensive national planning was also abandoned, the public sector was no longer subject to the same political and social considerations to which it had previously been subject. As a result of all these developments, the share of the public sector's contribution to total GDP declined quite fast: from 54.5% in 1974 to 49% in 1979.

The Privatisation that Never Was!

Although the intention was expressed of wanting to sell parts of the public sector to local investors, the idea actually never materialised. There are various views as to why this has been the case: some attribute it to the disinclination of Egyptian private capital to invest in productive activities, others to continuous resistance from personnel of the public sector towards this option. Although there is an element of truth in both, the main reason, in our view, is that the State and the bureaucratic bourgeoisie were not prepared to relinquish the control functions and the special privileges provided to them by a large, if transformed, public sector. Increasingly too, a major fraction of the State bourgeoisie became more interested in allying the public sector with international capital than in forming and strengthening ties with domestic capital.

Two major proposals in 1980 for selling the public sector to domestic capital therefore came to nothing. One was a proposal by Abd al-Razzaq Abd al-Majid, an ex-Minister of Economy, to turn public companies in the field of foreign trade and insurance into branches of mixed (public and private) holding companies. The other proposal was prepared by Taha Zaki, ex-Minister of Industry, and aimed at involving local private capital in the existing and the new industrial public companies. This latter attempt might have been partly a response to growing accusations that infitah had turned out to be basically consumer-oriented, since the emerging private investment concentrated on the areas of services, tourism, finance, trade, and real estate (from this derived the new slogan of the need for a "productive", not a "consumptive" infitah).

In 1981 a further proposal was announced, under the title of "separating ownership from management", whereby the ownership of the public sector would remain governmental and would be entrusted to a new National Investment Bank, which would in turn establish holding companies that would manage the capital of mixed (public/private) companies. Around the same time a similar concept was applied in the tourism sector, where two public companies in that field became "owning" but not managing companies, as they leased their hotels and assets to six foreign investment companies (joint foreign and public shared). During this period too, several important public sector companies were left without any boards of directors in anticipation of what might become of them.

Yet another new proposal emerged in 1982 for the establishment of new agencies of coordination and control (rather reminiscent of the previous "public organisations" of the Nasserist era) to advise the ministers concerned on the activities and profitability of companies belonging to them.[25] One further proposal then emerged in 1985 for "rationalising" the public sector, whereby all "loss-making" companies, as well as all public companies in domestic trade and tourism, would be liquidated and turned over to the private sector. The proposal was more or less accepted by Parliament in 1987. According to this idea, the public sector would keep only the large companies in productive areas such as textiles and minerals. The euphoria over privatisation even reached the point of a ludicrous proposal to sell the Suez Canal to foreign investors in order to repay Egypt's debts!

None of these proposals for selling the public sector has been carried through, but there is no doubt that the overall shift in the State's economic policies has meant that an already overburdened public sector is getting fewer resources for renewal of machinery, retention of qualified personnel, and so forth, at a time of growing competition resulting from the liberalisation of trade controls and the special exemptions and privileges given to infitah projects. Since the adoption of infitah, the ability of the public sector to generate surplus has certainly declined. Thus, although capital investment in the public sector had increased from £E4.25 billion in 1975 to £E31.98 billion in 1985 (i.e. six-fold), distributable surplus generated by the sector had only increased from £E435 million in 1975 to £E1376 million in 1985 (i.e. three-fold), all at current prices.[26] Put differently, surplus in 1975 represented over 10% of capital invested, while it declined in 1985 to only one percent of the capital invested.

There are two possible ways of interpreting this information: either the public sector was so inefficient that it could not withstand any foreign or private competition under the open door policy, or that it had become so badly neglected and starved of resources under infitah that decline was inevitable. Although the first proposition may be partly correct, there is sufficient evidence to support the view of the second school of thought as a main explanation for the decline. For the public sector was not really so inefficient: in 1976 the number of public sector units making profits was 324, while only 44 units were recording losses, amounting to no more than £E80 million (and their number was in any case on the decrease). Furthermore, during those same ten years (1975-1985), the State extracted an average 67.5% of the distributable surplus of the public sector (27.2% in the form of income tax and 40.3% in the form of "appropriation"), thus depriving public companies of the use of these funds for self-financing and for renovation and improvement.[27] Even so, the public sector did not collapse completely: in 1984/85, 83 profitable companies showed a combined profit of £E268 million, while 34 remaining companies showed a combined loss of £E142 million, for a net profit of £E126 million.[28]

Impact on Performance

The application of infitah policies has no doubt helped in solving some of the technological (i.e. production) problems of the public sector, and in easing some of the liquidity bottlenecks (especially with regard to foreign currency). The basic problem of finance has not been solved, however.[29] In addition, marketing has become an acute problem (because of opening up the local market to the severe competition of foreign products and because of disrupting the established trade with the Socialist countries).[30] Furthermore, the retention of qualified and skilled personnel has also become quite difficult, as many of these people leave the public sector to work either in other Arab countries, or in the local private sector, native and foreign.[31]

Infitah has also harmed the public sector in another indirect way—by fuelling large-scale corruption. This is to a significant extent a function of the emergence of a substantial private sector, with better financial resources, alongside the existing public sector which is structurally exhausted and financially starved. Constraints of space do not allow a full treatment of this subject, but I have dealt with its causes and manifestations elsewhere.[32] Corruption had to a large extent been ''institutionalised'' in the seventies, partly as a safety valve for the badly paid bureaucracy, and partly as an accompanying symptom of the laissez-faire policy. A number of trials in the early years of the Mubarak era revealed some horrendous cases that included the most notorious of all, that of the ex-President's brother, 'Ismat al-Sadat. From a humble driver and clerk, working in Alexandria's dock area, he ended up as a millionaire, achieving this elevation through all kinds of manoeuvres to exploit the linkage points between the public and the private sectors that included illegal dealings in licences and permits, trading in land, machinery, ships, factories, petroleum, food products and, some even say, drugs.

The summary abolition of the Administrative Control Agency in June 1980 was related in many people's minds to this and to other cases of grave corruption that the agency had been investigating. Their confidential three-volume report on cases of deficiency and deviance within the bureaucracy in the period 1970 and 1977, published at the end of the seventies, had obviously antagonised several high-ranking personalities. The Court's verdict confirmed that 'Ismat al-Sadat and other members of his family were involved in cases of fraud, black market trading, misappropriation of public funds, and many others (from a list of 24 accusations). This case, and others like it, threatened to be not only a case of corruption but ''a trial of a whole era''[33]—the implications were too threatening to the regime, and the series of corruption trials was brought to a rather hasty close.

Productivity versus Development

The broader subject of development at large cannot be dealt with in the available space–some shorthand statements will have to suffice. Shifts in the economic role of the State following the introduction of infitah, even assuming that they would have led to some improvement in productivity here and there, have not actually enhanced development at large. Indeed, the transformations currently taking place have meant that the State is conceding its leading developmental role and is instead accepting an increasingly "dependent" status vis-a-vis international capital. Even in the narrow sense of economic growth, infitah has not really been especially successful. Admittedly, GDP had grown at an average rate of about 8.4% per annum in the period from the mid-seventies to the mid-eighties, compared to an average of about 6.6% per annum during the period from the mid-fifties to the mid-sixties. However, whereas most of the growth achieved in the fifties and sixties was due to expansion in industry and other productive sectors, most of the "growth" under infitah was derived from foreign, *rentier*-type resources over which the Egyptian state has had very little control, and which are in any case known to be dwindling. Indeed, with the current decline in these resources, the annual rate of growth is already dropping, to less than one percent per annum by American estimates and less than five percent per annum according to Egyptian estimates.[34] In addition, the following figures for the eighties have to be taken into account: an annual rate of inflation of about 23%; an annual budget deficit of about $3.5 billion; an annual trade deficit of about $8 billion; and an accumulated debt to date of around $50 billion.

Conclusion

What general conclusions can be derived from the previous analysis? The following may at least be worth pondering:

First; that, quantitatively, retrenchment of the State bureaucracy is an extremely difficult (impossible?) task, even if ideological and policy changes point in its direction.

Second; that a relinquishing of the economic role of the State bureaucracy does not necessarily, immediately, and proportionately, correspond to a decline in its political (control and repression) functions.

Third; that productivity and development are not one and the same thing: the factor productivity of enterprises may rise while overall national development may falter.

Fourth; that terms such as infitah, liberalisation, and privatisation, do not always signify genuine deregulation, but sometimes "obscure a complex process of constructing new regulatory regimes intended to make both the State and a range of private corporate actors more 'market-oriented'", often under the impact of international forces.[35]

NOTES

1   This figure is very controversial, but tends in our view to lend itself to great exaggeration (owing among other things to the non-distinction between "stock" and "flow"). The 1986 census indiated 2.2 million Egyptians (out of a total of 50.4 million) resident abroad. The Minister of Emigration and Expatriate Egyptians, however, indicates that some 4.5 million

Egyptians were working abroad in 1986/87, of which 2.5 million were registered with Egyptian consulates. It was assumed that some 3 million were working in Arab countries alone.

2   From 1985, the State's commitment (inherited from the Nasserist era) to employ all graduates, albeit normally around three or four years after graduation, has been somewhat watered down. Government and public sector units are now expected to fill their vacancies through advertising and "competition"—only the residue is then centrally distributed through the Manpower Ministry.

3   Sources for this section of the study include: Ministry of Finance; Ministry of Manpower; National Bank of Egypt; Central Bank of Egypt; Central Agency for Public Mobilisation and Statistics (CAPMAS); State Information Authority; daily newspapers.

4   Cf. Nazih Ayubi, *Bureaucracy and Politics in Contemporary Egypt* (London: Ithaca Press, 1980), Ch. 3.

5   Many central government employees are located in branches all over the country and therefore count as "local officials" although they are not strictly speaking local government officers. The number of "local officials" in 1980 was 1,218,000. Ibrahim A. 'Umar and M. Saif Al-Shirbini, "Idarat al-mawarid al-bashriyya..." [Manpower Management in the Egyptian Administration], *Al-Idara*, Vol. 14, no. 1 (July 1981), 96-111.

6   'Adil Ghunaim, *Al-namudhaj al-misri li ra'simaliyya al-dawla al-tabi'a* [The Egyptian Model of Dependent State Capitalism], (Cairo: Dar al-Mustaqbal al-'Arabi, 1986), 232-233.

7   Illustrative of the importance of the control and repression machine is the fact that in 1984, for example, no fewer than ten officers were appointed at the rank of "assistant minister" and thirteen at the rank of "security director" with the Ministry of the Interior. *Al-Ahram*, 13 May 1984.

8   Ghunaim, *op. cit.*, 240-241.

9   See, for example, Nazih Ayubi, "Government and the State in Egypt Today", in C. Tripp and R. Owen, eds., *Politics and the Economy in Egypt Today* (London: Croom Helm, 1989) forthcoming; and Nazih Ayubi, "Local Government and Rural Development in Egypt in the 1970s", *Cahiers Africains d'Administration Publique*, no. 23, 1984, pp. 61-74.

10   Cf. Mark Cooper, *The Transformation of Egypt* (London: Croom Helm, 1982); and Raymond Hinnebusch, *Egyptian Politics Under Sadat*, (New York: Cambridge University Press, 1985).

11   John Waterbury, *The Egypt of Nasser and Sadat* (Princeton, NJ: Princeton University Press, 1983).

12   Cf. J. Waterbury, "The 'Soft State' and the Open Door: Egypt's Experience with Economic Liberalisation", *Comparative Politics*, October 1985, pp. 65-83.

13   The benefits of the open door policy were extended to the domestic private sector only by the "Companies' Law" No. 159 for 1981. By then, however, the native industrial entrepreneur was confronted with stiff competition from the emerging public sector/international capital joint ventures.

14   With meticulous documentary evidence (based on names, dates, assets, etc.), Samia Imam has illustrated that members of the bureaucratic bourgeoisie now form an important segment of the infitah "new class". They are mainly involved in the fields of foreign trade, contracting, "commercial agency" work and other financial activities where they may sometimes compete with and sometimes ally themselves with the prerevolutionary (capitalist) bourgeoisie. Members of the bureaucratic bourgeoisie came later than the traditional "capitalist" bourgeoisie to the business of forming and joining companies, their open activities becoming obvious mainly in the period following 1978 when the political leadership had most unequivocally given up its socialistic rhetoric. Samia Sa'id Imam, *Al-Usul al-ijtima'iyya li nukhbat al-infitah* [Social Origins of the Infitah Elite], MSc. thesis (Cairo University, Faculty of Economics and Political Science, 1986).

15   Cf. Mourad M. Wahba, *The Role of the State in the Egyptian Economy: 1945-1981*, unpublished D.Phil. thesis (Oxford University, 1986).

16   Central Auditing Agency, cited in *Al-Ahram al-Iqtisadi*, no. 842 (4 March 1985), p. 54.

17   Cf. Hazim al-Biblawi, "Al-dawla wa mujtama' al-muwazzafin" [The State and the Com-

munity of Officials], in *Al-Ahram*, 30 November 1987; Ali A. Sulaiman, "Al-mujtama' al-misri wa dawlat al-muwazzafin" [Egyptian Society and the Bureaucratic State], *Al-Ahram al-Iqtisadi*, no. 4942, 2 February 1987.

18   See for details: 'Adil Husain, *Al-Iqtisad al-misri...* [The Egyptian Economy from Independence to Dependency], (Cairo: Dar al-Mustaqbal al-'Arabi, 1982).

19   Cf. Nazih N. Ayubi, *Al-dawla al-markaziyya fi misr* [The Centralised State in Egypt], (Beirut: Centre for Arab Unity Studies, 1989 forthcoming).

20   Cf. Waterbury, 1983; M. G. Weinbaum, *Egypt and the Politics of US Economic Aid* (Boulder, Colo.: Westview Press, 1986).

21   Amani Qandil, "Jama'at al-masalih..." [Interest Groups and their Influence on Economic Policy], in *Al-Ahram al-Iqtisadi*, no. 850, 29 April 1985, pp. 16-17.

22   For details cf. Nazih Ayubi, "Implementation Capability and Political Feasibility of the Open Door Economic Policy in Egypt", in M. H. Kerr and E. S. Yassin, eds., *Rich and Poor States in the Middle East* (Boulder, C.: Westview Press, 1982), and references cited therein.

23   Fu'ad Mursi, *Masir al-qita' al-'amm...* [Destiny of the Public Sector in Egypt], (Cairo: Markaz al-Buhuth al-'Arabiyya, 1987), 19-20.

24   Central Agency for Public Mobilisation and Statistics, *Nata'ij hasr wa istiqsa' al-'amala fi majal al-idara...* [Results of the Full Survey of Management Personnel in the Economic Activities Sector in the ARE], (Cairo, 1974).

25   The public organisations (*mu'assasat*) of the Nasserist era were not as constraining on the productive activity of public companies as many believed. Their relationship to their affiliated companies was characterised by "qualified authority" rather than by "complete authority"—i.e. that for any decision by the public organisation there was not only one choice for the company but a set of alternatives available in executing a corporate decision. Cf. Salah Farid, *Top Management in Egypt* (Santa Monica, Calif.; The Rand Corporation, 1970), 37-38. The abolition of the "public organisation" formula in the seventies proved unsuccessful as it removed an important vehicle of direction and coordination. The practice had to be reintroduced, this time under the title of public authorities, *hay'at 'amma*, in the field of various industries, construction, transportation, agricultural and animal resources, housing, chemicals, foreign trade, and several others. Cf. Arab Republic of Egypt, *Qararat ra'is al-Jumhuriyya bi insha' hay'at al-qita' al-'amm* (Cairo: Al-Matabi' al-Amiriyya, 1984).

26   Mursi, *op. cit.*, pp. 29, 33.

27   *Ibid.*, pp. 8, 49.

28   American Embassy in Cairo, *Egypt: Economic Trends*, December 1986, p. 13.

29   Cf. Ibrahim Al-'Isawi, *Fi Islah ma afsadahu al-infitah* [On Repairing what Infitah has Ruined], (Cairo: Kitab al-Ahali, 1984), 129-146.

30   Cf. the various constraints listed in: National Specialised Councils, *al-Qita' al-'amm...* [The Public Sector: Constraints and Development], (Cairo, 1981), 10 ff.

31   It must be admitted that job satisfaction was not very high among the public sector managers. In the Central Agency for Public Mobilisation and Statistics (CAPMAS) survey (1974) referred to above, 74% of the managers believed that there were other posts that were more appropriate to their qualifications and experience, and 65% of the managers thought that their salaries did not correspond to their expertise and to their costs of living.

32   Nazih Ayubi in Kerr and Yassin, *op. cit.*, and Nazih Ayubi, "Bureaucratic Inflation and Administrative Inefficiency: the Deadlock in Egyptian Administration", in *Middle Eastern Studies*, Vol. 18. no. 3, July 1982.

33   'Abdallah Imam, *Muhakamat 'Asr...* [The Trial of an Era: the Case of 'Ismat Al-Sadat], (Cairo: Dar Rose Al-Yusif, 1983).

34   Economist Intelligence Unit (London): *Egypt: Country Profile 1987-88*, and sources cited therein.

35   P. Cerny and J. Jensen, "Deregulation, Re-regulation and the International Dimension", proposed workshop for the *European Consortium for Political Research*, (Paris, 10-15 April 1989).

Bureaucracy and Development in Syria:
The Case of Agriculture

RAYMOND A. HINNEBUSCH

College of St. Catherine, St. Paul, MN, U.S.A.

ABSTRACT

This article examines the Syrian bureaucracy through a case study of its role in agricultural development. It analyses the degree of technocratic rationality imparted to agrarian policy, the effectiveness of the bureaucracy in carrying out agricultural policy, the beneficial role of the bureaucracy for the agrarian economy and the peasantry, and the political consequences of the Syrian bureaucracy's role in agriculture. It also indicates that while senior public officials play a role in shaping agrarian policy, this role is in turn shaped by Ba'thist ideology and a political structure that vests control over high policy in the Presidency and the ruling party and not in the ministerial bureaucracy. This arrangement influences agricultural planning, administrative leadership, and patronage politics. This paper concludes that despite the flaws that afflict the agrarian apparatus, the Syrian bureaucracy has put in place development programs of great benefit to agriculture.

THE SYRIAN BUREAUCRACY OPERATES in a special political environment which shapes its role in agrarian development. In its radical phase (1963-70), the Ba'th Party tried to make the bureaucracy an instrument of socialist revolution from above. The radical phase initiated an etatist strategy of development which translated into steady expansion in the functions and size of the agrarian bureaucracy. It was charged with carrying out land reform, forging peasant cooperatives, and replacing landlord and merchant in the agrarian economy. Under Asad, as power and stability displaced radical change in elite priorities, the bureaucracy retained a central role in agriculture: it plans crop rotations, introduces technical innovations, delivers credit and services, markets crops, and manages land reclamation, irrigation, and agro-industry. It has assumed a more technocratic orientation, but it has also become an instrument of cooptation and a font of patronage, to the detriment of rational task performance. Total state employment has grown from 22,000 in the late fifties to 250,000 in the seventies to 473,285 in 1984 when one in every five persons was so employed, including 153,000 government officials, 92,000 teachers, and 130,500 public sector workers (SAR 1984: 88, 94); the agrarian bureaucracy has proliferated at a similar rate.

This essay will examine Syrian bureaucracy through a case study of its role in agricultural development. Do technocrats impart rationality to agrarian policy? How effective is the bureaucracy in carrying out policy? Is it a burden or a benefit for the agrarian economy and the peasantry? What are the political consequences of its role?

II. Ideology, Technocracy, and Agrarian Policy-Making

The technocrats of the senior bureaucracy play a role in the shaping of agrarian policy, but it takes place within a milieu shaped by Ba'th ideology and a political structure which centers power over "high policy" not in the ministerial bureaucracy, per se, but in the Presidency and the ruling party. The collegial Ba'th party leadership, the Regional Command, proposes, under presidential guidance, broad policies which are ratified by periodic party congresses. These policies are formulated by the command's array of specialized offices with responsibility for different policy sectors; the *Maktab Fallahin*—Peasant Office—is most directly responsible for policy on agriculture. The policies of the offices are, in turn, not made in a vacuum but coordinate, under a senior party apparatchik, the work of the various ministerial officials and interest group leaders—the Peasant Union in the case of agriculture—in their policy fields.

Party agrarian policy is most immediately shaped less by technical or economic rationality than by a mix between the persistence of statist-populist ideological preferences and the requisites of power. While the embourgeoise-ment of the power elite has been accompanied by a retreat of ideological motivation from elite circles, a residue of ideology is institutionalized in the Ba'th party and defended by party apparatchiki. Its imprint is unmistakable in the constancy with which the regime has pursued socialist-like solutions in agriculture, particularly cooperatization, and in its abiding distrust for private sector "feudalists" and merchants. The calculus of power generally reinforces étatist and populist policies: the state has a vital interest in state control over agricultural decisions and resources and in keeping the bourgeoisie—where political opposition is concentrated—from recovering its influence over the sector. And Ba'thist legitimacy is seen to rest on a state development effort exemplified by hydraulic projects and agro-industrialization. The subordina-tion of economic rationality to the calculus of power is evident in policies such as the use of the bureaucracy to maximise employment and in the sacrifice of profitability in agro-industry to patronage and low-priced output.

The state bureaucracy, in which the development orientation of the technocracy and the rational-legal traditions of career officialdom mix with patronage politics, does have an input into party decisions and their concrete application. There is plenty of evidence of the technocratic mentality in the policy process: debates over the matching of ends—self-sufficiency, greater productivity—and appropriate means, statist or market, the stress on planning of the agrarian sector, the drive to manage the environment through hydraulic projects or protection of the *badiya* (range or steppe), the deployment of new bureaucratic instruments meant to control and stimulate agriculture—all bear the imprint of this orientation. Technocrats arguing for economically rational adjustments in policy carry growing weight, their arguments being most effective when they promote a state interest in improved resource mobilization. But technocratic rationality by no means coincides with the promotion of market strategies at the expense of statism. Most technocrats accept the rationality of a major role for the state. The limits and abuses of development under the bourgeoisie before 1963 generated attitudinal support for expansion of the state sector. Once this began, investment by the alienated agrarian bourgeoisie largely ceased and, given the lack of resources and initiative among peasants, only state intervention could prevent stagnation and spur development. The strategy of the regime was at heart bureaucratic: if there was a problem or a need, create a new ministry or "general organization" to deal with it and, once created, vested interests became attached to these organizations. Where technocrats are divided, it is over the relative extent and purposes of the state's role. Those educated in the Eastern bloc view it positively as an instrument of both economic growth and socialist ideals. Other technocrats, especially those who are not the products of Ba'thist politicization, have diminished faith in the efficacy of the state's role and more in the market and private enterprise and they are strengthened to the extent "socialist" schemes, like state farms, have failed. The need to choose appropriate tenure forms in the reclaimed areas of the Euphrates is illustrative of the current balance of opinion within the elite: the alliance between party elites and Eastern-educated state bureaucrats in favor of production cooperatives and state farms reflects an enduring ideological bias in the regime; but its growing pragmatic willingness to experiment with other forms, such as service cooperatives and joint venture investment companies, indicates a technocratic flexibility likely to increase as resource constraints give ever greater weight to immediate-term economic arguments over ideological ones. But up to now, ideology and technocracy have worked in tandem giving a powerful étatist thrust to agrarian policy-making.

III. Planning in Practice: Technocracy in Action or Empire Building?

Étatism depends on the effectiveness of state planning and although Syria still lacks sophisticated planning mechanisms, planning is the main instrument through which agrarian strategy is translated into operational targets and implemented.

The Higher Planning Council, an inter-ministerial body headed by the Prime Minister, is the supreme decision-making body in the planning process. It formulates the general targets of the plan and is the arena in which ministries and agencies fight for their share of the investment budget. The planners, per se, are in the State Planning Commission (SPC) which provides the long-range studies and designs the macro-economic framework behind production targets and investment decisions, but it has lacked the means—sufficient data and expertise—to effectively play this role and the design of the plan results as much from the conflict of personal opinions and bureaucractic interests as from rational cost-benefit argument based on fact. Thus Syrian plans typically end up being a collection of goals without a rigorous specification of their interconnections and of mechanisms of implementation.

An elaborate agricultural production plan is designed which sets crop-targets and rotations tailored to various regions and the levels of inputs and credit needed to reach these targets. The plan is enforced through price policy, linkage of state credit to crop delivery, and by licensing of farmers. To cultivators, planning is an unwelcome constraint and "input" from below into plan formation usually insufficient to satisfy their wishes; they argue that they know best what to plant and that planning deprives them of the freedom to efficiently manage their farms. The "needs" of the country as projected by planners or imposed by party strategy rather than the wishes of the cultivators is often the decisive factor in the design of the production plan. Planners have tried to impose targets even against peasant resistance, e.g. sugar beet production, though they have to be flexible in enforcement since they cannot afford to alienate peasants for political reasons and peasants can always find ways of evading the plan. Government planning has had some success in reducing unnecessary fallow, stabilizing wheat output by concentrating it in good rainfall areas, diversifying crops, and getting farmers to grow and deliver crops needed for industry or export-crops they might otherwise not plant.

A state investment plan designed to support the production plan by channeling state resources into development projects and agrarian infrastructure is also formulated. Project identification and budget allocation emerge from a process of bureaucratic politics in which each agency is out to defend or expand its programs and the planning commission, lacking the authority to impose a coherent macro view on rival ministries, acts chiefly as a "recorder" or mediator of rival demands. The party apparatus has repeatedly imposed unrealistic land reclamation targets for the Euphrates Basin, expressive of its ideological stake in this showpiece of Ba'thism. Other projects are proposed by a ministry on the grounds that they fill a gap in plan implementation. But projects have been added by a powerful minister or party politician without benefit of any feasibility study by planners or even concern for the availability of financing—especially in the mid-seventies when the rival arms of the state apparatus were scrambling to claim a chunk of the Arab oil wealth pouring in. Perhaps the most infamous example of such a project is the paper pulp factory in Deir ez-Zor which was imposed by the Ministry of Industry against the opposition of the Planning Minister and which threatens to be an expensive white elephant. The belief that such project decisions have often been made as a result of commissions paid to high party and government officials is widespread.

Although the plan is legally binding in theory, in practice ministries regularly fall well short of their targets. This is partly because of unrealistic goals and partly due to uncontrollable environmental factors, such as technical problems with gypsum in the Euphrates project or shortfalls in Arab financial assistance caused by political conflicts. But much of the problem is due to bureaucratic and contractor mismanagement or inertia. Each ministry often goes its own way when the success of a project requires the cooperation of several. Monitoring of performance is weak. Problems are left to reach the crisis stage before any effort is made to cope with them; the result is bottlenecks—the need to stop projects because of scarcities of materials or imported equipment or unsynchronized completion of different project components. In the absence of sufficient data and expert analysis, follow-up sessions of the Higher Planning Council typically fail to pinpoint responsibility and degenerate into efforts by officials to justify their errors or defend their ministries. As bureaucrats get used to plan failure, the plan's value as a serious guide to action is eroded. Because planning doesn't work well, it does not follow that it is unimportant. It remains the basic arena for dividing up resources between competing priorities and interests. It is a way of periodically measuring performance and the major mechanism, feeble as it may be, for coordinating the multitude of government agencies. And it is developing, little by little, into an instrument for the control of resources which has strengthened the grip of the state over the economy.

IV. Administrative Leadership

The institutionalization of goal-setting in the party has given a certain consistency to the main lines of agrarian policy. But the regime has fallen down in translating goals into coherent enforced plans and in providing adequate resources to implement them. Indeed, the implementation of policy has often been characterized by incoherence and discontinuity.

The prime minister is the chief executive responsible for day-to-day policy implementation and through his council of ministers he formally presides over the vast ministerial bureaucracy. But he has insufficient authority over many of his own ministers and the council of ministers, its composition reflective of the intra-regime factional balance, is not a cohesive team devoted to getting a job done. "Each ministry acts as if it were an independent interest in conflict with the others" (Hilan 1973:113) and high officials often see only the interests of their own agency. The result is an enervating lack of coordination in policy implementation. Cabinets also undergo a fairly rapid turnover so that few ministers become masters of their policy domains. A major source of bureaucratic ills is, thus, the failure of political leadership to provide proper direction to the bureaucracy.

The weakness of the council of ministers is especially damaging for agriculture because responsibility for it is so widely dispersed across the bureaucracy. While the Ministry of Agriculture and Agrarian Reform has chief responsibility for implementation of agricultural policy, it lacks direct authority over many other agencies crucial to its mission. The Agricultural Bank, crop export agencies such as the cotton marketing agency, and the foreign trade bodies which import agricultural inputs are subordinated to the

Ministry of Economy and Foreign Trade. The Ministry of Internal Trade regulates market prices for agricultural goods and controls the General Organization for Cereals Marketing and Processing which buys much of the grain harvest. The Ministry of Industry controls the food, textile, and sugar firms which buy and process crops and the industries which produce farming inputs such as fertilizers and tractors. Coordination is supposed to be achieved by the Higher Agricultural Council (HAC), a body chaired by the Prime Minister and including the heads of these agencies, which translates the Five Year Plan into yearly implementation plans. The Minister of Agriculture also presides over an implementation sub-committee of the HAC, which is supposed to have authority over other ministries in their agriculturally relevant operations down to the village level. But the HAC lacks sufficient authority to overcome fragmentation and, indeed, at times lapses into inactivity and the Agricultural Ministry lacks sufficient weight in inter-ministerial arenas to supervise implementation effectively, although much depends on the political stature of the minister and whether he enjoys the backing of the head of the *Maktab al-Fallahin* and hence of party power.

Indeed, in a political system where authority is highly centralized and personalized, the quality of leadership is especially decisive for administrative performance. Unfortunately, the Agricultural Ministry has suffered from a lack of strong, consistent, and appropriate leadership. Only two ministers have had extended tenure; one, Muhammed Haidar, was a corrupt politico lacking even an agronomy degree and the other, Ahmad Qabalan, had an agronomy degree and power, too, but did not have a reputation for putting the interests of development first. Other ministers have had short tenures or lacked agricultural expertise. Rapid turnover in ministers has been a continuing obstacle to continuity in decision-making. The lack of strong leadership means the agrarian sector comes out shortchanged in the struggle over resources and suffers from a lack of coordination, which translates into endless bottlenecks.

V. Patronage Politics

Between policymaking and outcomes exists a shadowy particularistic politics run along informal clientalist channels, carried on by *shillas* colonizing the legal institutional structures, aiming at private gain through public office. Such practices include official extortion of commissions on state contracts; according to insiders, agriculture ministers and their deputies have headed clientalist networks which take cuts on all such transactions. A number of high officials have personal or family businesses on the side to which they channel state contracts. Outright embezzlement of public funds or theft of goods happens. Indicative of the growing scope of corrupt practices is the fact that the major recent factional conflicts inside the agrarian bureaucracy have taken the form of rivalries between opposing coalitions of high officials and supplier agents over control of the contract tendering process and the commissions at stake in it. Indeed, the Ministry of Agriculture was rocked in the mid-eighties

by a struggle over contracts between the Minister, Mahmoud Kurdi, and his
Alawi deputy which ended in the fall of both. The pernicious effects of these
practices is obvious. A leadership engrossed in struggles over spoils is hardly
well equipped to lead a development effort. They drain the public treasury, at
the expense of tax-payers, of development funds. When patronage considerations displace rational analysis in the planning process and commissions dictate
the choice of projects, cost-benefit rationality goes by the board.

The securing of special privileges, exemptions to the law, or use of public
offices as sinecures for clients and kin are other typical practices. Licenses to
export livestock to the lucrative markets in the Gulf or to import agricultural
machinery and the right to rent extensive state lands in the East at low prices
are prized plums which agricultural authorities can distribute to clients. When
exceptions and exemptions from the law proliferate, planning and regulation
are subverted. One Minister of Agriculture was accused of illegally running
a large farm on marginal areas officially reserved for grazing; if the minister
himself encroaches on the *badiya*, how can his ministry protect its fragile
ecology? State cattle farms have been overstaffed several times to provide
sinecures for regime loyalists, subverting their mission to integrate cattle into
the agricultural cycle and, in ruining the farms economically, discrediting collective social forms.

On a yet more petty level, many local officials take bribes from peasants
to overlook regulations or insist on them as the price of the official approvals
or services peasants are formally entitled to or for prior consideration cutting
through red tape. The growing bureaucratic penetration and regulation of
agriculture has raised the costs of such practices for peasants. On the other
hand, well-placed persons can also use their position to help out kin in the
village: the case of a strategically-placed aide in the presidency who got the
agricultural ministry to drill wells and plant trees in his village is typical, not
exceptional.

VI. The Ministry of Agriculture and Agrarian Reform: Structure, Per-
sonnel, Pathologies

The transformation of high policy into practice requires all the skills of
rational-legal bureaucracy. The Ba'th's drive to enhance state capabilities
translated into a burst of organization-building and inexorable growth in the
functions, size, penetration, and real impact of state structures on agriculture
over the past decades. The agrarian bureaucracy was responsible for a long
series of reform and rationalizing innovations. The regime made major
breakthroughs in development of political-administrative technology needed to
bring policy to the village: land reform broke down traditional forces resistant
to state penetration, cooperitization institutionalized state linkages to peasants,
and an array of specialized bureaucratic organizations were deployed to carry
out policy tasks. But the efficiency of the state apparatus has failed to keep pace

with its structural expansion and it is thus riddled with "pathologies" which enervate its performance.

The structure of the Ministry of Agriculture illustrates both the range of tasks and the multitude of pathologies typical of the bureaucracy. The ministry is run with far too little delegation of power, overburdening the minister and the 29 department heads reporting directly to him is an excessive span of control. As a result, decisionmaking is sluggish and initiative by subordinated discouraged. There is a complex but haphazard division of labor at ministry headquarters. The minister and his three deputies preside over an array of specialized *mudirat*—directorates. Directly under the minister is the strategic Administrative Affairs Directorate which controls budgeting, accounting, contracts, personnel matters, and inspection. Under the First Deputy Minister are key directorates such as Planning & Statistics which prepares and supervises plan implementation and collects data on its outcome; and the Directorate of Agricultural Affairs which determines input needs and supervises their delivery. Also within his responsibility are sectoral directorates in charge of plant protection, forest management, soils (surveys, classification land use planning), and three autonomous offices, the Cotton, Olive and Citrus bureaus, which perform research, quality control, and marketing functions for these crops. Also under his supervision are functional directorates for agrarian reform and state property management, extension, and supervision of agricultural secondary schools. A second deputy minister responsible for research supervises the agricultural research stations. A third deputy minister supervises sectoral directorates chiefly responsible for livestock—animal husbandry (breeding, fodder supply), animal health, *badiya*, range and sheep management, and rural building and machinery. Finally, several autonomous state production or commercial enterprises, including state farms, the Ghab administration, and the General Organizations for Cattle, for Poultry, for Fish, for Fodder, for Seeds and for Agricultural Machinery report directly to the minister. This structure, which developed piecemeal, lacks a consistent basis for the division of functions and suffers from an overlap of responsibilities among directorates. The operation of the central ministry is also hampered by a tendency to set general goals without a proper design for implementation and evaluation, for delimiting jurisdictions, and for setting standards and measures of job performance. Officials often identify solely with their directorate instead of with the ministry mission. According to a critique of the agronomists' syndicate, there is a failure to "give those with responsibility appropriate power, especially in cases where they must co-ordinate several functions which have to be done simultaneously since delay in the performance of one leads to a chain of bottlenecks in the performance of others". Too many administrators are mere "protectors of the rules" rather than expediters of task performance. There is an excessive stress on hierarchy and the chain of line command, expressive of too much concern for power prerogatives and not enough for the kind of interaction and communication needed to get a job done.

At the *muhafazat* (governorship) level is a *mudir al-zira'i* (agricultural director) on the staff of the governor who coordinates field offices corresponding to the central level directorates; his staff agronomists are supposed to be specialists consulted by lower level field workers. At the *mantiqa* (district) level is an "agricultural head of service" in charge of several agronomists and "agricultural assistants". At the lower *nahia* (sub-district) and cooperative levels, agronomists and cooperative supervisors are supposed to preside directly over field services and regulation. One major defect in this structure is the weak communications between levels. Specialists do not communicate directly with other specialists at higher levels but must go through the line executive at the higher level; thus plant protection specialists in the governorate communicate with their directorate in Damascus through the minister's administrative office. Since line executives are overburdened, the result is damaging delay. The ministry has also failed to establish a sufficient field presence: as late as 1976, 66% of government agronomists were located in province capitals, 16% in the districts, and only 8% in the *nahias*. While this has since improved, the lack of housing and of the transport needed to keep local officials mobile continue to afflict the bureaucracy. Moreover, technical experts have to devote much of their time to administrative tasks such as licensing, crop reporting, and enforcing regulations. Both the motivation and opportunity to get agricultural officials out of their offices and into the fields with farmers have been lacking.

The bureaucracy also suffers from acute personnel problems. There has been a severe scarcity of technically competent personnel. No College of Agriculture even existed until 1960. In 1965, Syria had 400-500 agronomists (*muhandis zira'i*), the basic technical cadre, and by 1977, there were 3,000, but the country needed at least double that. While the numbers of technical cadres (*kadr al-fanni*) have grown rapidly, as new specialized government services expand, the demand for specialists has run ahead of availability, in good part because the university agronomy course is devoid of specialized training. In 1968-69, only 58 agronomists in Syria had advanced degrees (e.g. in livestock or olives); ten years later the state employed only 225 cadres with such degrees. Worst of all, the quality of agronomists and other technical cadres is often mediocre. The agronomy faculty does not attract the very brightest students, faculties and facilities are inadequate, and training is too academic, providing little practical experience; farmers often discover they know more than the recent graduates sent to instruct them. New appointees to the agrarian bureaucracy begin work in their own districts, and a bonus is paid for work outside Damascus; but agronomists of urban background find it hard to adjust to field work and resist assignment in the countryside. Many personnel practices also produce low levels of motivation. Only too frequently, the right man is not put in the right post. Advancement by seniority may contain favoritism, but in not rewarding achievement, promotion is forfeited as a spur to performance. Salaries, especially in senior positions, are low compared to those in the private sector and outside Syria. The four to one range in basic salaries between the lowest and highest grades in the bureaucracy is commendably egalitarian, but it leads to a brain drain from senior positions. Low salaries generate an obsession with bonuses and allowances but because these often depend on individual pull or the power of an agency, they are often arbitrarily distributed. Generally, agricultural agencies and especially the ministry have been disadvantaged in the race for such extras; the resulting sense of discrimination is very damaging to motivation in the bureaucracy. Inflation is, however, the most corrupting and enervating threat to the integrity of the public service; it reduced the real salaries of senior officials in the agricultural ministry by 64% from 1974 to 1979 and in the mid-eighties had worsened significantly. This obviously encourages corruption among those in a position to trade decisions or services for money. The irony is that government's own deficit financing has contributed to the inflation which debilitates its own capabilities.

VII. Outcomes: The Developmental Consequences of Bureaucratic Intervention in Agriculture

The multitude of flaws and pathologies which afflict the agrarian apparatus translate into a great amount of waste and inefficiency. Yet, an analysis of actual policy outcomes suggests that, given enough time, the bureaucracy has put in place and carried on programs of great benefit to agriculture.

The first major undertaking of the Ba'thist regime was land reform. Syrian agriculture had reached an impasse, caught between semi-servile labor on low productivity estates and capitalist proletarianization. Land reform demolished the latifundia, checked the proletarianization of the peasantry and effected a major leveling in the agrarian structure. It broadened and consolidated the small holding sector, creating a mixed small peasant and medium capitalist agrarian structure at the cost of only temporary declines in production. Indeed, the post-reform agrarian economy, in enhancing peasant independence and initiative, increasing the incorporation of the peasant into the market, and forcing greater investment by landlords on their reduced holdings, is more dynamic than the old latifundia. Yet, in eschewing a more thorough equalization of land holdings and permitting the preservation of medium sized estates, the regime failed to make enough land available to wipe out landlessness and consolidate a secure middle peasantry.

The cooperatives were the crucial linkages between the peasantry and the agrarian bureaucracy needed to make land reform viable. The regime has indeed succeeded in organizing a large portion of the small peasantry into a cooperative framework which channels resources, services, and innovation to the small holding sector, deters land reconcentration, and excludes landlords and merchants from major channels of sectoral interchange. Far from being economic failures, cooperatives have upgraded the small peasant sector which would otherwise be fatally vulnerable. But they have generally failed in their more ambitious mission as building blocks of agrarian socialism: they organize little collective investment and few of the common production processes needed to overcome land fragmentation. As instruments of government control, often putting state interests first—as in compulsory planning and the practice of collective responsibility for debts—the cooperatives have not won peasant confidence and as village institutions they have failed to overcome the mutual mistrust of an individualistic or familistic peasantry. In providing no ''socialist'' alternative, they leave the road open to a return to agrarian capitalism. Indeed, cooperatives, in fostering individual peasant development, may be generators of a rich or middle peasant capitalism.

The state's planning, credit, and input system has advanced the regime's control over production decisions, while providing peasants with relatively cheap access to the credit and inputs needed to stimulate productivity and intensification and to break the control of usurers over the village. The bureaucracy has initiated a score of useful innovations, from orchard development, seed and animal improvement to mechanization, but the dismal performance of the research and extension apparatus is an obstacle to their proper design and delivery to peasant producers. In constantly allowing planning and coordination to lag behind its initatives, it generates ever new kinds of bottlenecks. When one seems on its way to solution—e.g. delivery of fertilizer—another one emerges as the economy becomes more complex—e.g. fodder delivery. State marketing has given the regime reasonably effective control over strategic crops, such as cotton and wheat, essential for export earnings and food security, while also guaranteeing producers stable, if not exactly lucrative markets, but is has yet to effectively organize the delivery of raw materials to produce processing factories.

More direct government interventions in agricultural development and production have a mixed but poorer record. The apparent failure of state grain farms seems to mean the decline of an alternative to the resurgence of ''merchant-tractorist'' agrarian capitalism on the great eastern plains. The state hydraulic record is only a little better. The Ghab irrigation project, long ''sick'' from incompetent state management, is finally operative and has transformed an area of desolation and urban dominance into a viable peasant community with a certain prosperity. The much more ambitious Euphrates project is, in an arid country which has reached the limits of extensive expansion, a natural next step in agricultural development. It could reproduce the Ghab outcome but has so far been a costly drain on the state's limited resources and a strain on its modest management capacities. Generally speaking, massive investment in irrigation and reclamation has done little more than prevent a backsliding in the amount of irrigated surface instead of advancing Syrian agriculture beyond its crippling dependence on unreliable rainfall.

The overall economic outcome of state intervention in agriculture is mixed. The state has fostered intensification and mechanization with considerable success. There has been a continuous increase in agricultural production. A growth in agricultural per capita output, despite a decline in the agricultural workforce, indicates that agriculture is being brought to support a growing non-agricultural population—a symptom of advance toward structural transformation of the economy—but it has not overcome the deficit in the agricultural balance of trade. This record is certainly not compatible with any generalized claim that the state is an obstacle to development. But, for better or worse, the agrarian bureaucracy has not become an effective engine of capital accumulation. Not only has it failed to extract much of a surplus, generally subordinating the profit motive to the servicing of agriculture, but it dissipates resources on salaries for an oversized officialdom and through corruption and inefficiency.

The public sector has developed some of the crucial sectoral interchanges which stimulate development. Industry provides inputs, markets, and employment opportunities which have helped stimulate agriculture, while the construction sector provides hydraulic public works and the transport infrastructure needed to integrate village and market. But agro-industry, the very nexus of the sectoral interchange, embodies a fatal flaw in the state's development effort. Agro-industries are victims of all the pathologies of the regime: politicized, incompetent, underpaid and undermotivated management, an undisciplined work force, a turning of factories into patronage fiefdoms, and the subordination of profit to social-political objectives—maximization of employment, consumer price stability, self-sufficiency. Agro-industry has thus failed to mobilize the capital for its own reproduction and has been unable to meet consumer demand and sustain development without costly dependence on outside capital.

VIII. Bureaucracy and Peasant: The Social Consequences of State Intervention

Has state intervention in agriculture burdened and exploited or benefited the peasant? A "bureaucratic state bourgeoisie" has certainly emerged at the top of the bureaucracy enriching itself at the expense of the public treasury. The proliferation of bureaucratic personnel and corrupt official extractions from peasants, are, moreover, symptoms of parasitism. But most of the bureaucratic middle class, far from enriching itself, suffers from low salaries. Nor has the bureaucracy become a instrument for the exploitation of the peasantry. Even the state marketing system, a potential instrument of extraction, has not been systematically so used. Indeed, a stable state market and subsidized credit relieve peasants of the old threat of debt and expropriation and the ruinous fall in crop prices typical of the free market, providing a basic security which would be rapidly missed if the state withdrew from this role. The state—in the form of services, credit, and investments in irrigation and land reclamation—is probably putting more *into* agriculture than it extracts. There are conflicts of interest between the bureaucratic elite and the peasant: the former seeks control—e.g. in the imposition of crop rotations too often indifferent to the interests of the peasants—while the latter seek to maximize their independence. But the allilance between agriculture ministry bureaucrats and peasant union leaders in pursuit of higher producer prices does not square with the notion of a basic state—peasant cleavage.

At the local level, the bureaucracy constitutes one of the main structures linking state and village. Although the potential for arbitrariness is diluted by the plurality of local authorities—party, peasant union, ministry officials— who take decisions in committees, peasants are sometimes the victims of arbitrary power exercised in the absence of strong legal or customary checks on officials. The recruitment of most officials from the village itself gives some of them sympathy for village problems, but others are more interested in escaping from their background and dislike having to work in the field. There is a gap between the self-interest of the local bureaucrat and that of the peasant: "the peasant is dependent on production; (the bureaucrat's) salary is fixed. He has no need of the people, is not responsible to them, so the quality of his work declines, he lacks a sense of duty and works mechanically (Tal)." But the typical local bureaucrat is not part of a new class standing against the peasant or the instrument of the local landlord, and peasants are no longer passive victims. Many find ways to evade, even manipulate the state: a son will join the local party, a bribe will sway an official. Patronage is "democratized" at the local level as public goods are diverted and laws bent to favor locals. Thus, the intervention of the state has brought opportunities and resources, not just constraints and extractions.

The cumulative social impact of state intervention in the agrarian economy is three-fold. For the most part, it has favored producers, consumers, and the bureaucracy at the expense of the landlords and merchants who have been cut out of a lucrative source of wealth on which their prosperity was historically raised. Second, the formerly rigid class structure which kept the village encapsulated has been broken, superseded by a much more permeable one. The state has stimulated enough development to permit peasants to diversity their resources, e.g. by taking advantage of new opportunities for off-farm income and of state-provided credit and inputs to intensify production. Rural life has become more viable, and the cultural and opportunity gaps between city and village have narrowed. Petty peasant accumulation seems to be growing out of an increased prosperity. Third, state intervention has pluralized power at the village level, breaking the former fusion of wealth and power in the hands of the local landed élite. The lines between rich and poor peasants have also probably been blurred by state intervention since, in diversifying peasant opportunities, it gives less favored peasants chances to remedy their resource scarcity. The result seems to be a less, not more rigid agrarian structure. In practice, the activity of the state seems to have two faces: it burdens and constrains agriculture but overall it has done more to serve, stimulate, and protect the peasant. This is not, of course, necessarily the final outcome and, faced with a resource crunch, the regime might yet turn on the peasantry.

IX. Conclusions: The Political-Economic Consequences of Ba'thist Agrarian Development

The primary political consequence of the agrarian development launched under the radical Ba'th was the incorporation of the peasantry into the regime by state penetration of the village, the wider dispersion of property and services the regime brought to it, and the growing access to education, state employment, and patronage made available for rural youth. The Ba'th regime displayed a greater ability to foster change in the village than most authoritarian regimes and the consequences for agriculture and the viability of the village were generally positive.

But the Ba'th seems to have reached the limits of its social engineering capacity. It exhausted its rural mobilization capacity without having created viable institutions which could substitute for capitalism. The growing limits of statist development must inevitably start to reshape agrarian policy, most likely bending it in a more overtly capitalist direction. The embourgeoisement of the top power elite could create the conditions for a capitalist transformation of elite ideology, while growing peasant entrepreneurship and the accumulation of private capital in the village as well as the city could provide the objective conditions. Persistent populist ideology, entrenched statist interests, and the growing corrupt and arbitrary use of official power at the expense of legal-rationality constitute major obstacles to capitalist development. But the costs of state intervention in an era of growing patrimonialization are likely to exceed benefits and a contraction of the state in favor of markets and private enterprise to be forced on it by tightening economic constraints and new social forces.

BIBLIOGRAPHY*

ARAB BA'TH SOCIALIST PARTY
  1972 *al-hizb wa al-masala al zira°iya* (The Party and the agrarian question). Damascus.
BAKOUR, Yehia
  1976 *A Study of Demand for Agricultural Engineers in the SAR in the Coming Stage to 1985.* Damascus.
  1978 *Supporting Policies and Services for the Agrarian Reform Program in Syria.* Damascus.
  1984 *Analytical Study on Major Changes in Agrarian Structure and Land Tenure Systems in Syria.* Damascus: Arab Organization for Agricultural Development.
BIANQUIS, Anne-Marie
  1979 "Les Coopératives Agricoles en Syrie: l'example de l'oasis de Damas," *Revue de Géographie de Lyon,* n. 3.
HILAN, Rizk-allah
  1973 *Suriya bayna al-takhallof wa al-tanmiya* (Syria between Backwardness and Development). Damascus.

* This select bibliography indicates some of the sources for the analysis. A more thorough documentation of the claims in the essay may be found in the author's *Peasant and Bureaucracy in the Ba'thist Syria: The Political Economy of Rural Development* (Westview Press, 1989).

HINNEBUSCH, Raymond A.
  1976 "Local Politics in Syria: Organization and Mobilization in Four Village Cases,"
      Middle East Journal, v. 30, no. 1, Winter, pp. 1-24.
  1982a "Rural Politics in Ba'thist Syria," *The Review of Politics*, v. 44, n. 1, January, pp.
      110-130.
JUMA , na`im
  1972 *Dirasa tahliliya muqarana li waqi' mazra'a dawlah wa jam'iya ta'awuniya zira'iya wa
      mazra'a khassa* (A Comparative Analytical Study of the Condition of State Farms,
      Agricultural Co-operatives and Private Farms). Damascus.
KHADER, Bishara
  1975 "Propriété agricole et réforme agraire en Syrie," *Civilisations*, n. 25, pp. 62-83.
METRAL, Françoise
  1980 "Le monde rural syrien à l'ère des réformes (1958-1978)." in André Raymonde,
      et al. *La Syrie d'aujourd'hui*. Paris: CNRS, pp. 69-89.
  1984 "State and Peasants in Syria: A Local View of a Government Irrigation Project,"
      Peasant Studies, v. 11, no. 2, pp. 69-89.
SYRIAN ARAB REPUBLIC, Central Bureau of Statistics
  1984 *Statistical Abstract, 1984*. Damascus.
TAL, Muhammed Fayez
  1967 *al-Mujtama' al-'Arabi as-Suri fi al-Dawla al-Haditha* (Syrian Arab Society in the New
      State). Damascus: Dar al-Ta'awun.
U.S. DEPARTMENT OF AGRICULTURE, USAID, and Syrian State Planning Commission
  1980 *Syria: Agricultural Sector Assessment*. Washington, D.C., 4 vols.
WAZZAN, Salah
  1967 *Min al-Takhallof illa al-Tahwil al-Ishtiraki fi al-Qita al-Zira'i* (From Underdevelopment
      to Socialist Transformation in Agriculture). Damascus.
ZA`IM, Issam
  1967 "Le problème agraire Syrien," *Développement et Civilisations*, no. 31.

Bureaucracy and Development in Jordan

JAMIL E. JREISAT

University of South Florida, Tampa, FL, U.S.A.

ABSTRACT

Bureaucracy is the major instrument of socio-economic development in Jordan. It functions within an environment of scarce resources, overpowering political leadership, and particularistic cultural habits. This study reviews not only the progress made towards achieving the goals of national development but also the obstacles that retard modernization efforts. It examines specific bureaucratic pathologies in the Jordanian political-administrative structure: clerkism, centralism, nepotism, incompetence, and the negative effects of such factors on development and administrative effectiveness. The examination of official administrative reform efforts in Jordan indicates that the substantive issues of reform have not been effectively articulated or managed.

T HE STUDY OF ADMINISTRATION and development in Jordan reveals the many contrasts and disparities of a small, modernizing country striving to achieve ambitious plans for development in an economy of scarcity. Jordan was catapulted into statehood by British colonial rulers after Worl War I, as the state of Transjordan. For centuries this territory, with Palestine and Lebanon, was associated as part of Greater Syria. British and French colonial orders tore the region into zones of influence in the secret agreement between them known as the Sykes-Picot treaty of 1915.

International events and pressures continued to dominate the evolution of the country, which became known after 1950 as the Hashemite Kingdom of Jordan, more than any domestic exercise of any power. This fact largely explains the image of precariousness and volatility many analysts continue to ascribe to Jordan in times of prosperity as well as in times of economic and political stress (Jureidini and McLaurin, 1984; Satloff, 1986). Nevertheless, under conditions of economic scarcity and, occasionally, political upheaval, Jordan managed an impressive social and economic development at the domestic level which achieving greater influence at the international level than seems warranted by its natural resources, size, or military power.

The system of government is fairly differentiated and many of the functions of the administrative, political, legislative, and judicial structures are constitutionally articulated. The executive branch is headed by the king, who exercises his authority through the prime minister and the Cabinet. As Richard Nyrop (1980:160) points out:

"The monarchy remains the most important institution in the country. The king appoints the prime minister, the president and members of the Senate, judges, and other senior government and military functionaries. He commands the armed forces, approves and promulgates laws, declares war, concludes peace, and signs treaties. The king convenes, opens, adjourns, suspends, or dissolves the legislature; he also orders and may postpone elections..."

This analysis focuses on the Jordanian bureaucracy and the socio-economic development of the country under the constraints of scarce resources, a dominant political leadership, tribalistic and personalized culture, and the continuing effects of the Palestinian-Israeli conflict. The indispensable role of mangement in socio-economic development is examined in order to define problems and delineate future policies and directions.

Development

For more than three decades, development planning has been the key instrument of socio-economic change in Jordan; therefore, the development plan became the overall framework for directing public and private energies and activities. Various planning techniques have been practised at various times, such as planning for single projects in the 1950s to comprehensive planning in the 1960s and, more recently, a combination of sectorial and national socio-economic planning (Five-Year Plan, 1987).

From the beginning, the country was confronted with a combination of factors largely beyond its control. One is limited natural resources. Only six percent of the land is arable, no oil has been discovered, and water supplies are inadequate. Another is the adverse effects of hostilities in Palestine since 1948 leading to a dramatic increase in population as displaced Palestinians fled to Jordan and defence expenditures increased. These are two major and persistent problems that development plans have had to contend with over the past four decades.

However, in the early years, Jordan was able to build a basic infrastructure, establish a number of small industries, implement a large irrigation project (the East Ghor Canal Project), expand the education and health services, and develop and upgrade the institutional and administrative framework for development. Figures showing economic growth from the early period (1952-1966) are impressive by comparison, i.e., the annual growth rates of gross domestic product (GDP) at market price was 6.9% and for gross national product (GNP) was 7.5%. In the second period (1967-1972), the pace of growth slowed down to 4.6% GDP and 4.2% GNP, mainly as a consequence of the 1967 war and the military cost (Five-Year Plan, 1987:3,9).

The first Five-Year Plan (1976-1980) was formulated under conditions of increasing Arab financial assistance and loans during the oil boom and the growing demand for Jordanian manpower in the Gulf countries. Between 1973 and 1981, Jordanian exports jumped 12-fold, and remittances of 350,000 doctors, engineers, and construction workers in the Gulf states reached one billion dollars annually (Satloff, 1986:9). These favorable economic accomplishments revitalized economic growth as they led to a dramatic rise in consumption and imports.

Robert B. Satloff (1986:8) describes the effect of the oil boom during this period as follows:

> "Between 1973 and 1981, Jordan enjoyed a remarkable economic boom. In that period, the kingdom consistently registered real annual growth rates (GNP) of around 9-10 percent; gross domestic product (GDP) increases averaged 8 percent per year. Gold and foreign exchange reserves increased 6-fold; capital formation increased 11-fold—all in a country with little more than a drop of oil to its name."

Nevertheless, economic indicators point out some serious problems constraining comprehensive development in Jordan. For example, increasing reliance on Gulf states for economic assistance and labor markets have bound the Jordanian economy to the economies of these states. The result is greater uncertainty and less control over the directions of domestic development. Furthermore, according to estimates by The World Bank (1987), the increase in central government expenditures reached 43% of GNP in 1985 and the growth of external debt reached 71% of GNP in 1985. Along with these factors a dramatic increase in consumption and imports intensified the troubles ahead for comprehensive development. Having Jordan committed to wide-ranging capital expenditures and development projects, the country may now find itself dangerously overextended (Satloff, 1986:2).

But economic indicators, such as GNP, alone are inadequate to define or measure the more complex process of comprehensive development and modernization. In Jordan, as elsewhere in Third World countries, the concept of development has evolved from a narrow focus on activities and projects that increase the national income to become a broader definition of development that accords proper emphasis to social and cultural considerations. This shift of focus is reflected in the literature, where the word "development" today signifies societies' struggle against poverty, unemployment, and impediments to social justice and equality. As a result social indicators, distributional effects of policy decisions, employment objectives, and other consequences of developmental programs are more prominent in national development plans (Jreisat, 1986).

Development in Jordan has been relatively comprehensive and socially conscious. Various development plans reflect concerns that extend beyond the typical industrial, agricultural, and public works projects that dominate traditional plans. The current Five-Year Plan (1986-1990) deals with the environment, public administration, labor, women, youth, culture, and social aspects as well as service, infrastructure, and productive sectors. The objectives and values to be served by the various indicators are indicative of the new and expanded commitments of public policy makers.

It does not mean, however, that the inclusion of a proposed activity in a development plan is a guarantee of its implementation, as the experiences of the Third World countries amply illustrate (Rondinelli, 1982:47). The actual performance of Jordanian development planners and the review of publishing planning documents clearly reveal certain predicaments and deficiencies:

First, domestic financial resources and the current tax base in Jordan are inadequate to finance any ambitious development plan. ''Domestic revenue provides little more than half the government's expenditure; direct taxes account for less than one-tenth'' (Satloff, 1986:26). Consequently, development financing has always been tied to external considerations of borrowing and assistance—a situation permeated by a sense of tentativeness and suspense throughout the span of the plan. With the growth of external debt from 24-71% of GNP between 1970 and 1985 (The World Bank, 1987:237) and significant reductions in foreign-assistance receipts, an environment of uncertainty and speculation shadows public policy decisions.

Second, a noticeable deficiency in the planning process (which culminated in the Five-Year Plans) is the absence of needs assessments and real information to authoritatively define what is needed, what has been accomplished, and what policies and actions are proposed for the future. The development plan often read like a shopping list with a price tag that seems to signify funds control rather than policy commitment, cost, or any meaningful measurement of activities. It appears that neither impact analyses nor needs assessments have been introduced into development plans.

Jordan's poor census procedures do not help, either. Except for published numbers of job applications to the Civil Service Bureau in Amman, no one knows exactly how many Jordanians are out of work, for example. Mass unemployment and lack of job openings cause greater strain on the fragile Jordanian economy than any other of its myriad financial woes; nevertheless, Jordan's ''manpower and employment statistics are uniformly poor'' (Satloff, 1986:29, 30).

Third, management is considered ''the single most important determinant of economic growth'' and ''a major cause of retarded economic growth in developing countries'' (Yavis, Kaynak, and Dilber, 1985:29). In Jordan, the lack of mangerial competency has been frequently cited as the main reason for the poor record of implementation of earlier plans (Mazur, 1979). The most recent Five-Year Development Plan recognizes certain administrative and organizational problems the country faces. It lists several proposed projects and measures to improve administrative performance and to develop managerial skills at the national and local levels. This appropriate attention indicates increasing awareness of the importance of the managerial capacity to implement such a plan.

Once more, the proposed administrative measures and projects in the plan are devoid of empirical content, reasoned justification, or assessment of expected outcomes at any level of tentativeness. The general approach is basically of the traditional, legal genre of prescriptions that lack an action orientation, conceptual sophistication, or substantive relevance; hence, they are old remedies of proven inadequacy (Jreisat, 1988).

Finally, a great deal has been written about the need to decentralize the legal and political authority to plan, make decisions, and manage public functions from the central government and its agencies to their field organizations, local authorities, or even nongovernmental organizations (Rondinelli, 1981:137). In the meantime, evidence from Third World countries indicates that success stories of decentralization are very rare (Graham, 1980:231; Rondinelli, 1981 and 1982). For example, in Jordan as well as in most Arab countries, new laws were passed since the 1950s to reorganize local authorities to achieve decentralization and expand the role of local authorities in the development process. Very few of these objectives actually materialized and the results of the decentralization policies have been disappointing (Jreisat, 1980).

Therefore, any advocacy of decentralization must be tempered with a greater sense of realism and broader understanding of the range of options as well as the contextual characteristics of such policies. Specifically, we must recognize the presence of certain factors justifying, perhaps, a moderate measure of centralism, particularly when governments are compelled to reduce or stabilize expenditures, achieve a higher discipline, and reach greater consistency of policy in a developmental expansionist environment (see Shick, 1988:524).

Thus, the issue of centralization/decentralization in Jordan has political and administrative justifications on either side of the argument. However, adaptation of the process of public decision-making is essential to conform to socio-economic changes inspired by the spread of education, the expansion of the urban segment of the population, the decline of tribalism, and the growth in personal income. Overcentralization and the continuation of a highly particularistic mode in governmental policies and actions are less appropriate to current conditions in Jordan. "Top-down" systems of decision-making that do not allow for political participation and for flexibility in adapting to local conditions are inconsistent with the rapid modernization of a society that has been unfolding over three decades. Societal change is complex and interrelated, consisting of movements and alterations that frequently develop a momentum of their own. Therefore, the Jordanian authority system cannot indefinitely prevent the devolution of certain powers and the allowance of greater freedoms of expression, association, and participation in public affairs.

In brief, the political culture in Jordan that has facilitated a virtual free hand for the political leadership not only in political matters, but also in economic and administrative decisions, has rendered salient questions about who benefits by public policy and the nature of the process that determines those policies (Jureidini and McLaurin, 1984; Satloff, 1986; Nyrop, 1980).

Administration

Public administration in Jordan, as in Third World countries, is crucial if developmental plans and policies are to be implemented. Government is dominant and overreaching in all aspects of society. Public expenditures are close to half of GNP at the present and civil servants have increased 300% in 15 years—27,000 in 1970 to 74,000 in 1985—(Five-Year Plan, 1987:121).

In comparison with other developing countries, the Jordanian bureaucracy usually inspires less negative characterizations and sometimes is commended for its performance. In a message to his prime minister (June 18, 1984), the King of Jordan referred to public employees as "key to development" and a "model to be emulated in many Arab countries." Throughout their brief history, Jordanian bureaucrats have had the benefit of basic education, exposure to other managerial practices—mainly Western—and numerous reorganizations based on professional consultants' studies and evaluations. Training activities within the country and abroad, along with the availability of formal education at the university level, offered public employees further opportunities for personal growth and professional development.

Despite these various attempts at professionalization, the performance of the Jordanian bureaucracy remains constrained by a particularistic style of decision-making at all levels. Over the years, tribal loyalties have been a more powerful focal point of identification and action than loyalties to the state (Jureidini and McLaurin, 1984:4). Nepotism and favoritism are common practices as public decisions are made. Citizens cannot predict the outcome of a specific public decision based on facts alone because it often depends on the weight of pressures brought to bear on the officials by friends, family members, or associates in favor of one side or the other.

Social life in Jordan centers largely on the family. In principle and usually in practice, the individual's loyalty to family overrides other obligations. The good repute of the family brings honor and dignity to its members beyond personal achievement (Nyrop, 1980:82). Geert Hofstede (1984:83) refers to this cultural dimension as "collectivism" which stands for a preference for a tightly knit social framework in which relatives and in-group members exchange favors and loyalty. Education, urbanization, and mobility have slowly begun to alter or modify perceptions, attitudes, and customs that subordinated the individual to the family and clan. However, such change is not at the level where universalistic principles of merit and due process are superseding personal ties in governmental actions, for example.

Another characteristic of the Jordanian bureaucracy is an excessive overcentralization of authority. The Five-Year Plan (1986-1990:123) describes the problem this way: "Too much centralization in certain agencies, where the agency head becomes the sole decision-maker on most issues, coupled with a responsibility span which is too broad for effective management." In a survey of senior public managers, centralization of administrative authority was identified as the number one problem of the organizational structures of their offices; lack of delegation of responsibilities was the second (Al-Khadra, 1980:34, 80).

As indicated earlier, ideological advocacy of decentralization has not produced hoped-for results. Consequently, before recommending remedial measures, a more realistic approach requires the identification of the organizational contexts of overcentralization, its causes, and its consequences.

In Jordan, certain readily identifiable factors accentuate the tendency toward centralization within the system:

(1) Scarcity of resources breeds greater "top-down" control over any decisions with financial implications;

(2) Jordan is a small country, with about half of its population and more than 93% of its economic enterprises employing five persons or more located in the capital city (Abu-Shaikhah and Assaf, 1985:43); hence, centralization is made easier;

(3) A history of political control that centralizes authority at the top has conditioned successive generations of over-compliant administrators seeking to patronize the political order; and

(4) The level of administrative skills among middle and lower level managers, many of whom reached their positions through particularistic means and operate at the upper limits of their competency, forces more and more responsibility for decision-making to higher levels in the hierarchy.

But excessiveness in centralization has its price. Administrative bottlenecks, underutilization of time and talent of supervisory staff, low level of innovation and preoccupation with red tape, encouragement of influence peddling by citizens who know how to "go to the top" for all matters with government are some of the reported consequences (see Palmer, et al., 1987). Heads of departments rule their units as chiefs of tribes; they hold all powers, real and symbolic, irrespective of performance considerations, employees' morale, or citizens' satisfaction.

The irony of the matter is that these heads of departments themselves are constrained by excessive control tendencies at the Cabinet and the prime minister levels. Policy matters, allocation of resources, and even senior personnel matters are routinely referred to the prime minister or the minister for action.

Consequently, clerkism replaces leadership, and preoccupation with small and routine matters preempts concern for overall policies of the organization. In a survey of 345 upper- and middle-level Jordanian administrators (sponsored by the Institute of Public Administration), most respondents did not answer the questions asking them to define some of the organizational problems they face and to suggest solutions. Only 15% of the respondents offered their views on how to solve the problems. The interpretation of the researchers who conducted the survey was that the administrators "lack the time or possibly the capability to think of the problems facing their organizations and to develop long-range plans for solving the serious ones" (Al-Khadra, 1980:33).

Thus, the Jordanian bureaucrat is a hard-working clerk who enjoys the certainty of the routine and the job security of public employment. The challenge of innovation or the concern for overall policies are, perhaps, at the outer limit of their managerial skills and political risk-taking. The attitudes of the administrator operating as a clerk—unmindful of the larger questions— have been fostered and institutionalized among Jordanian managers first by the colonial system and later by the current, overcentralized government. Lucian Pye (1969:410) points out how the colonial administration demanded infinite attention to detail and inhibited imagination, achieving a remarkable uniformity of the product in the colonies.

Administrative Change and Development

The short-term prospect of major departures from the prevailing administrative pattern in Jordan is unlikely. The situation is further complicated by the spreading and deepening of some of these tendencies and behavioral patterns in the bureaucracy and by the citizens, producing greater challenges to those who would undertake the task of administrative reform.

Administrative reform has been a part of the political agenda of every prime minister in Jordan since the 1960s. The impetus for reform drives and the process of initiating them (and legitimizing their results) are similar. The prime minister and Cabinet or the king himself order a study of a certain administrative problem, or administration in general, to recommend change. International consulting groups then become the vehicle for such a study, or a commission on administrative reform is established, with members chosen from among select local political and administrative groups.

International consultants' reports, for example, resulted in the initial civil-service law of the country and many of its amendments. The Griffin-Hagen Kroger Study examined organization and procedures at ministries and other government institutions in 1966. Two years later, a Ford Foundation study suggested the establishment of the Institute of Public Administration. The World Bank and McKinzie Consultants Study reported a system of follow-up during implementation of the Three-Year Development Plan starting in 1973 (Five-Year Plan, 1987:122).

Also in the 1970s, several national committees were established to suggest administrative changes. The Royal Commission for Administrative Development, ordered in 1984 by a royal decree, has received the greatest publicity and national attention. Chaired by the prime minister, its members include ministers, technocrats, and academicians. Its mandate is to provide a comprehensive examination and evaluation of the administrative system and recommend improvements.

This Commission has focused on three administrative dimensions:

(1) The government's current organization and relations among public agencies;

(2) The comprehensive national law governing the civil service;

(3) The various operative financial laws of the country.

The Commission has come up with specific recommendations in each of these areas, recommendations which are to be made public. The Institute of

Public Administration is to provide detailed programs of action for implementation (Rifa'e, 1987).

The Jordanian perspective on administrative reform appears to be evolving since the early 1970s. In the early part of this period, reform was defined in terms of alterations involving organizational structures, procedures, and work methods. These changes were to take place through the establishment of an organization-and-methods (O & M) unit, located in the budget office. This O & M unit sought to fulfill its responsibilities through procedural changes, drawing new organization charts, and streamlining the flow of work (Adwan and Ellayan (1986:41).

The O & M approach was abandoned in 1972, however, in favor of a committee for reorganization that pursued its objectives through changes in the law and the regulations of governmental agencies. This committee also attempted to reduce bureaucratic red tape, end duplication of responsibilities, and suggest actions to further the goals of administrative development (Adwan and Ellayan, 1986).

Preliminary assessments of these early efforts of administrative reform indicate conceptual narrowness and an uneven record of implementation. The narrowness derives from a preoccupation with efficiency factors perceived in terms of procedural and legal modifications of managerial practices. No significant changes in the power distribution within and among agencies were attempted and no attention was paid to the importance of affecting values and attitudes of administrators. Change was approached in a fragmented way; efforts seemed to be advancing without clear goals and lacked coordination with national development plans.

In contrast, most recent administrative reform efforts demonstrate greater sophistication and maturity. Serious attention is given to integration of administrative development plans with the national comprehensive development plan, for example. The Royal Commission of Administrative Reform is to provide political support for the necessary activities and recommendations. The Institute of Public Administration and the Civil Service Bureau are sponsoring workshops to engage the administrative and political leaderships in a dialogue over the reform mandate, its approach, and its recommendations (Ellayan, 1987).

The views of the Jordanian senior bureaucrats, however, reveal dissatisfaction with the organizational settings as well as with the overall administrative performance of their own agencies. A 1987 survey of 76 departmental heads and permanent secretaries indicates that only 23% of the respondents (12 out of 52) expressed positive opinions when asked: ''Do you consider the organizational structure suitable for the goals and activities of your department?'' In the same suvey, 27% said they had no programs of administrative development in their organizations; 36% expressed dissatisfaction with their employees' performance; 52% indicated their departments lack adequate information systems; and 56% admitted that their services do not meet citizens' expectations (Ellayan, 1987).

These results are significant because they represent the views of the "bureaucratic elite" in Jordan and because they indicate a higher level of negative assessment than was found in earlier surveys of other groups of public managers (see Al-Khadra, 1980). The most striking feature of the 1987 survey, also sponsored by the Institute of Public Administration, is the absence of any questions requesting input or suggestions from these managers about the administrative shortcomings they identified. Whether this is because researchers lacked faith in managers' competency, found the issue politically explosive, or simply failed to employ adequate survey techniques is difficult to determine.

Conclusion

Jordan has been experiencing profound socio-economic change producing intense pressures on governmental institutions and processes. The increases in population and consumer spending, when agricultural land is shrinking and external sources of funding are drying up, intensify the economic pressures faced. The decline of tribalism, improvement of educational standards, and the growing attentiveness of the Jordanian citizen to public issues are forcing greater demands for modernization as well as for equitable and effective delivery of public services.

The choices for Jordan seem limited. Improving the political and administrative decision-making processes is unavoidable, if the country is to cross the margin of traditionalism to modernity. The administrative change hinges on building the capability and developing the professionalism of the Jordanian bureaucracy which is the most viable institution and the largest spender and employer in the society. This is the main reason why administrative reform has been prominent on the Jordanian public policy agenda.

Historical factors, cultural attributes, and characteristics of the system of government condition managers to behave as clerks rather than administrative leaders. Centralism, dictated by scarcity of resources and perpetuated by fears of corruption or political disloyalty, is a major contributor. Procedural reforms such as redrawing of organizational charts or amending of laws and rules in isolation from organizational realities, are inadequate responses which, by themselves, will not improve the performance of bureaucracy.

Administrative reform is contingent upon effective integration of various elements to create a coherent approach that is guided and monitored, not commanded or manipulated, by the central government. Such a strategy must include the following elements: (1) Flexibility and experimentation with innovative administrative processes such as privatization and deregulation, whenever feasible; (2) Vitalizing local authorities and institutions, which means encouraging local initiatives, providing training for local staffs, and devising techniques for greater local participation in developmental activities; (3) Improving public policy formulation and implementation, including establishing long-range, clear, and operational national objectives followed by short-range steps to design programs and allocate resources for achieving those objectives; and (4) Establishing "roadmaps" that make possible the gauging of an agency's progress and success in implementing its tasks. This involves the development of high quality accounting data, disclosure of public commitments, and reliable reporting on the performance of all governmental programs.

Finally, decisive to the accomplishment of administrative reform in Jordan is the exercise of political will to provide genuine support for administrative improvements that attempt to achieve equitable public decisions, curtail bureaucratic corruption, and stimulate local initiatives. Public policy outcomes that favor the few among politicians and bureaucrats and administrative changes that are merely technical and procedural manipulations lose not only legitimacy but also their value to national development.

REFERENCES

ABU-SHAIKHAH, Nader and A. M. ASSAF
> 1985   *Public Administration in The Hashemite Kingdom of Jordan* (in Arabic). Amman: Jordanian Press Institute.

ADWAN, Yaser and Abdullah ELLAYAN
> 1986   "Jordan's Experience in Administrative Reform," *Asian Affairs* VII, I: 40-56.

AL-KHADRA, Basheer
> 1980   *The Status of Public Organizations in Jordan* (in Arabic). Amman: Institute of Public Administration.

ELLAYAN, Abdullah
> 1987   "Report: Conference on the Role of Higher Administrators in Administration Development" (in Arabic). Amman, Jordan: Institute of Public Administration, 1-21

ESMAN, Milton
> 1988   "The Maturing of Development Administration," *Public Administration and Development* 8, 2 (April-June): 125-134.

GRAHAM, Lawrence S.
> 1980   "Centralization versus Decentralization Dilemmas in the Administration of Public Service," *International Review of Administrative Sciences* 46, 3:219-232.

HOFSTEDE, Geert
> 1984   "Cultural Dimensions In Management And Planning," *Asia Pacific Journal of Management* (January):81-99.

HUDSON, Michael
> 1977   *Arab Politics: The Search for Legitimacy.* New Haven, Conn.: Yale University Press.

JREISAT, Jamil
> 1988   "Administrative Reform in Developing Countries: A Comparative Perspective," *Public Administration and Development* 8, 1 (January-March): 85-97.

JREISAT, Jamil
> 1986   "Introduction" in J. E. Jreisat and Z. R. Ghosheh (eds.), *Administration and Development in the Arab World: An Annotated Bibliography.* New York, NY: Garland Publishing.

JREISAT, Jamil
> 1980   "The Fertile Crescent Countries," in Donald E. Rowat, ed., *International Handbook on Local Government Reorganization.* Westport, Conn: Greenwood Press.

JUREIDINI, Paul and R. D. McLAURIN
    1984 *Jordan: The Impact of Social Change on the Role of the Tribes*. The Washington Papers,
        108, Vol. XII. New York, NY: Praeger.

MAZUR, Michael
    1979 *Economic Growth and Development in Jordan*. Boulder, Col.: Westview Press.

MINISTRY OF PLANNING, Jordan
    1987 *Five-Year Plan for Economic and Social Development 1986-1990* (in English).

NYROP, Richard (ed.)
    1980 *Jordan: A Country Study*, Foreign Area Studies. Washington, D.C.: The American
        University.

PALMER, Monte, *et al.*
    1987 "Bureaucratic Rigidity and Economic Development in the Middle East: A Study
        of Egypt, the Sudan and Saudi Arabia," *International Review of Administrative Sciences*
        53:241-257.

PYE, Lucian
    1969 "Bureaucratic Development and the Psychology of Institutionalization," in *Political
        and Administrative Development*, R. Braibanti, ed.. Durham, N.C.: Duke University
        Press.

RIFA ͨE, Zaid
    1987 "The Role of Administrative Leadership in Administration Development in Jor-
        dan," *Ash-shaeb*, Arabic Daily Newspaper (August, 17):10.

RONDINELLI, Dennis
    1982 "The Dilemma of Development Administration: Complexity and Uncertainty in
        Control-Oriented Bureaucracies," *World Politics* XXXV, 1:43-72.

RONDINELLI, Dennis
    1981 "Government Decentralization in Comparative Perspective," *International Review of
        Administrative Sciences* 47, 2:133-145.

SATLOFF, Robert
    1986 *Troubles on the East Bank: Challenges to the Domestic Stability of Jordan*. New York, NY:
        Praeger.

SCHICK, Allen
    1988 "Micro-Budgetary Adaptation to Fiscal Stress in Industrialized Democracies,"
        Public Administration Review 48, 1 (January-February): 523-533.

The WORLD BANK
    1987 *World Development Report 1987*. Washington, D.C.

YAVAS, V., E. KAYNAK, and M. DILBER
    1985 "The Managerial Climate in Less-Developed Countries," *Management Decision* 23,
        3: 29-40.

Political Culture and Development in a Rentier State:
The Case of Kuwait

TAWFIC E. FARAH

La Jolla, CA, U.S.A.

ABSTRACT

This article uses political culture to explain Kuwait's socio-economic and political develop-ment. It attributes Kuwait's political stability, its smooth transition from a subsistance economy to petroleum-induced prosperity and its ability to handle high rates of socio-economic changes to the management skills of the Kuwaiti ruling family and the commitment of the bureaucracy to the state. These two elements of political culture explain how the Kuwaiti regime has been able successfully to meet the challenges of development which would otherwise have made it a prime candidate for instability. The article concludes that Kuwait's political culture creates a bond between Kuwaiti citizens and their ruler, with the bureaucracy promoting and strengthen-ing allegiance to the state and its development policies.

IT WAS NOT UNTIL the oil "crisis" of 1973 and the rise of Khomeini in Iran in 1979 that interest in the Gulf and the Arabian peninsula changed pervasive indifference to the area into active concern. Academic interest fol-lowed political concern. Professors would supply policymakers with the "recipes" to contain revolution and maintain the status quo. Academic interest in the societies and politics of the Gulf is also part of a general interest in politics and economic development in the Third World. The theories advanced in the West to describe Third World politics and development seem inadequate. They may be elegant, but they somehow lack the empathy needed to understand politics in these societies[1].

Kuwait is a case in point. How do these theorists explain the stability of this political system, and the country's smooth transition from a subsistence economy to petroleum-induced prosperity? Dizzying rates of economic and social change have not been accompanied by political dislocations. The al-Sabahs have been at the apex of this political system for more than 250 years and remain there at a time when governing monarchs are a dying breed. If credit is not due to their political and management skills during boom times, it is fully due for these skills in times of economic contraction. How has this system managed so well? Where can we look for an explanation of this success story: in the modernization literature, in the dependency literature, or perhaps in the political culture literature? But first a look at the system itself.

II

Kuwait became fully independent in 1961, when the 1899 agreement that gave the United Kingdom responsibility for its foreign policy was terminated. The constitution adopted a year later vested executive power in an hereditary Emirate, with succession fixed among male members of the al-Sabah family, and created a National Assembly of fifty members, elected for four-year terms.

Kuwait is a very small and closed political system, governed by the Emir, Jaber al-Ahmad al-Sabah, who is the "father" and the "patron" of the Kuwaiti family. He shares some of his powers with the inner councils of the ruling family and the elders of the leading merchant families: al-Qatami, al-Nisf, Boudai, al-Ghanim, al-Saqr, al-Khorafi, al-Bahr, al-Shaya, al-Roumi, al-Mula, al-Marzooq, al-Khalid, al-Badr, al-Saleh—all Sunni Muslims who control most of the banks, large companies, and import agencies. A couple of Shi'a families, including Behbahani and Quabazard, have access to the inner sanctums of decision-making.

Kuwaiti politics can be lively and refreshing when compared to politics in other Gulf states. Yet, the press is censored, subsidized, and controlled by the government, and although the National Assembly engaged in lively debates before its dissolution on July 3, 1986, power still rested with the Emir, who could veto all laws. The National Assembly was a pressure group, an irritant, and a safety valve for the political system. (Participation in the national elections was, of course, limited to the approximately 350,000 male first-class citizens, and only 56,848 of them, or 3.5 percent of the total population, actually voted in the 1985 election[2]. Constitutional restrictions on voting were intended to exclude the 60 percent of the population that is non-Kuwaiti, including the many Bedouins whose traditionally nomadic lifestyle militated against their being able to meet constitutional requirements for Kuwaiti citizenship. Therefore, even though they make up half of the military and police force, they hold foreign passports. The safety valve is now shut off. Will political dissent, which is centered primarily on domestic issues, go underground with ominous implications for the al-Sabahs? or will it be managed?

The ruling al-Sabah family occasionally erupts in a feud. The battle lines in the struggle for power are drawn between the al-Ahmad branch (the Emir) and the al-Salim branch of the heir apparent (the crown prince), Sa'ad al-Sabah.

The al-Ahmad branch is represented by the Emir; the Deputy Prime Minister and Minister of Foreign Affairs, Shaikh Sabah al-Ahmad; the Minister of the Interior, Shaikh Nawaf al-Ahmad; and the Minister of Information, Shaikh Nasser Muhammad al-Ahmad; undersecretaries from the al-Ahmad branch sit at most of the key ministries and control the state security apparatus. Justice Minister Shaikh Salman Du'aij was part of this group before he relinquished his portfolio. The remaining al-Sabah in the Cabinet, Shaikh Salem at Defence, is politically inactive.

The sole representative in the cabinet of the al-Salim branch is the crown prince himself, who serves as prime minister. The oil minister, Shaikh Ali Khalifa, supports the crown prince.

Arab Nationalists formed an important bloc in the National Assembly. The Nationalist movement is led by Dr. Ahmad al-Khatib, who has been absent in the previous assembly but reemerged in the 1985 election. Ahmad al-Khatib's relations with the al-Sabahs blow hot and cold. His disappearance and reemergence in the National Assembly reflects both the status of his relationship with the government at that point and the government's ability to draw electoral districts for its own convenience. It is said that the government saw to it that the Nationalists were represented in the Assembly to balance the power of the Islamists.

Three members of the Nationalist group and eight who share some Nationalist views sat in the Assembly.

The thrust of the Nationalist program is economic. The Nationalists assail the government's failure to regulate and supervise the financial system and what they claim to be its mismanagement of the 1982 crash of the Souk el-Manakh (the unofficial stock market where foreign stocks were traded). On foreign-policy issues they are in general agreement with the government.

The Kuwaiti establishment contends that Islamic fundamentalism is on the wane. They point out that the Islamic groups, who were represented in the National Assembly by three hardcore Sunni fundamentalists and two or three sympathizers, and the Shi'a, who were represented by three members, lost ground in the National Assembly elections of 1985 and also have lost ground in professional associations and students' groups.

The al-Sabahs who demonstrate their fidelity to Islam have the backing of the *Ulema* (Muslim religious leaders). The *Ulema* receive generous support for religious education and for new mosques. They, in turn, support the al-Sabahs and help militate against any radical destabilizing influences.

Is this wishful thinking? While the government has a control handle of the "establishment" Islam and its bureaucratic apparatus, it does not control the general social and political movement generated from below by populist Islam. Of course, the growing power of populist Islam is not monolithic. There are Sunni as well as Shi'a dimensions. The Sunni fundamentalist movements are al-Salafis (traditional), al-Islah (reform), and al-Ikhwan (Muslim Brotherhood).

Populist Sunni Islam is a potent force in Kuwait (and also among Kuwaitis studying in the United States and the United Kingdom). Regardless of their divisions, all members share (1) a fundamentalist faith in the *Qur'an*, the prophet Muhammad, and the Sunna (tradition); (2) a strong opposition to corrupt and oppressive government; (3) a commitment to the related principles of human equality and social justice; and (4) a condemnation of external intervention in the Middle East. The adherents of populist Islam are willing to make a total commitment to their beliefs and, when called upon, to die for these beliefs. The government meets this challenge with an active security apparatus (including deportations) and by generous subsidies for buildings, new mosques, and various Islamic activities.

Populist Sunni Islam represents a challenge to the status quo, but it is more tolerated than its Shi'a in Kuwait number approximately 140,000 (some 20 to 24 percent of the population), and their community is bound together by a network of mosques, *diwanniyas,* and *husseiniyyahs.* Some are well-to-do (hence establishment Shi'a) but others remain hopelessly locked out of the corridors of power.

In the economic sector the regime has had a number of challenges which have been met with success.

The oil industry dominates Kuwait's economy, accounting for close to two-thirds of the GDP, and the end of the oil boom brought a drastic decline in oil revenues. There are problems, too, in Kuwait's meager industrial sector. The slackening of world demand for chemical products, combined with a shortage of natural gas for fuel, has led to a petrochemicals industry operating at far below capacity.

Despite the sharp drop in government revenues, Kuwait has managed so far to avoid serious inroads on its domestic budget by using income from investments made abroad, when oil revenues were flowing freely, to take up the slack. This allows the government to continue to fund the civil service bureaucracy, in which most Kuwaiti citizens are employed. But some austerity measures have been instituted (small payments are now required for medical care, for example).

The domestic economy is improving after suffering a few years ago from an acute lack of business confidence and a shift in consumers' liquidity. Erosion of private and public wealth in Kuwait as a result of the steadily falling prices on the Kuwait stock exchange, estimated to amount to a total of KD 7.2 billion, has been stemmed. Although Kuwait was an excellent candidate for instability—a shrinking economy, religious tensions, a regional war, Islamic fundamentalism and terrorism—the al-Sabahs have skilfully managed this witches' brew and kept it from boiling over. How? A look at the social science literature might be enlightening.

III

The modernization literature which dominated the study of the Third World, including the Middle East, posited the dichotomy of tradition/modernity. Nations and individuals were either modern or traditional. Progress was linear—from one extreme, tradition, to the other modernity. There were connections between capital accumulation, economic growth, social mobilization; and these, of course, led to demands for political participation. Once the genie was out of the bottle, we were told, it would be hard to put it back—or how are you going to keep them down on the farm after they have seen Paris![3]

Modernization literature has been attacked for theoretical and empirical reasons, and an alternative approach—dependency theory—has been introduced. This theory drew a connection between the international economic and geopolitical systems in the center on the one hand, and the form of rule in the periphery on the other. Dependency literature focuses on the importance of oil, for example, as a valuable commodity extracted in the periphery for the benefit of the center. But Kuwait is a country with a well-managed economy and a capital surplus. Its relationship with the center is more complex than a dependency theorist would have it[4].

A political culture approach focuses attention on the individual members of the society under study, their systems of political belief, their expectations and aspirations. A group of Arab political scientists at Kuwait University has written widely on the Kuwaiti individuals' "cognitive", "affective", and "evaluative" orientation toward the Kuwaiti system. We will attempt to distill their findings in an effort to explain their extraordinary capacity for survival and self-preservation under very adverse conditions[5].

IV

Political culture in Kuwait is also a function of its one-resource economy. Extracting oil involves a very few workers, who extract it and then sell it. Hence the rentier state[6].
As Mahdavy states:

> Rentier States are defined here as those countries that receive on a regular basis substantial [a]mounts of external rent. External rents are in turn defined as rentals paid by foreign individuals, concerns, or governments of a given country.... Oil revenues received by the governments of the oil exporting countries have very little to do with the production processes of their domestic economies.... The input requirements of the oil industry from the local economies... is so insignificant that for all practical purposes one can consider the oil revenues almost as a free gift of nature or as a grant from foreign sources[7].

This rentier state expends the rents and does not tax or extract revenues from the population. The state expends revenues on the elites and on the masses in a politically sophisticated formula.

The first mechanism the al-Sabahs used to transfer wealth to the elites was a land-acquisition program in which land largely owned by the elites was purchased by the state at inflated prices. The net effect of this transaction was a revenue transfer from the state to the elites. At the same time, the al-Sabahs generally stay out of the private sector, which is a small part of the economy[8]. Of course, the ruling family dominates the oil sector. Keep in mind that the elite merchant families have no domestic constituency of their own and are totally dependent on the al-Sabahs for their well-being.

Oil wealth has also trickled down to the poorest nationals. There is no question that the average Kuwaiti is better fed, better housed, better educated, and healthier than ever before. When a Kuwaiti compares his lot today with his lot prior to the oil era, he knows that he is much better off. When he compares his lot to the lot of his neighbors in other Arab states, he counts his blessings. Of course, this prosperity is a direct result of policies instituted by the al-Sabahs, policies which subsidize every aspect of dailey life, including employment. In this case it is not the state that puts demands on the people. It is the people who demand and expect a standard of living unrivaled in this part of the world.

As shown above, a bureaucracy was developed to distribute income and create employment. The state is then the employer of first and last resort[9]. Even employees in private banks owe their jobs largely to ownership stakes the government has in these banks and in other joint venture companies. Kuwait, for example, has seventeen ministries and almost a similar number of public institutions, employing approximately 150,000 civil servants.

The state bureaucracy is bulky. In a few cases there are examples of "rational bureaucracy" in the administration. However, to a large extent the civil service mirrors society: *wasta* and kinship permeate. Bureaucracy reinforces the traditional way of doing things and creates allegiance to the state. The bureaucracy does not extract taxes but distributes revenues. "May God bless the al-Sabahs" is a bureaucrat's way of showing gratitude to his generous employers, be he a university professor or a university custodian[10]. Furthermore, since the state does not need to create a coercive apparatus to extract revenues, it is not unduly overbearing as it would be in many neighbor states. It is usually the extraction of revenues that precipitates violence and opposition to the state, and it is the response to that opposition that creates strong states[11].

V

The achievements of the Kuwaiti political system are impressive. To understand these achievements, one has to emphasize the political skill and management of the leadership of this small but unique country. There is a "fit" between the political system and its political culture[12]. Because of the country's small size, access to its political system is achieved primarily through personal channels. Families still dominate the social and political life in Kuwait. The Kuwaitis have had a unique political experience. Freedom of expression has been to a great extent guaranteed. The system has been generous with its allocation of economic goods. When a Kuwaiti compares his lot to that of other Arabs, he realizes how well off he is.

The state endures. As Bernard Lewis has said, states have shown—even the most improbable of them—an extraordinary capacity for survival and self-preservation, often in every adverse circumstances[13].

NOTES

1   See John Waterbury, "Social Science Research and Arab Studies in the Coming Decade", El Sayed Yasin, "In Search of a New Identity of the Social Sciences in the Arab World: Discourse, Paradigm, and Strategy," and Judith Tucker, "Middle East Studies in the United States: The Coming Decade", all in Hisham Sharabi (ed.), *The Next Arab Decade: Alternative Futures* (Boulder, Col.: Westview Press, 1988). For a refreshing analysis of

Kuwaiti politics, see Khaldoun H. al-Naqeeb, *Al-mujtama wa al-dawla fi al-khalij wa al-jazirah al-arabiya* [Society and state in the gulf and Arabian peninsula] (Beirut: Center for Arab Unity Studies, 1987); Abd Allah Fahad al-Nifaisi, *Al-Kuwait al-raay al-akhar* [Kuwait: another opinion] (London: Ta-ha Advertising, 1978); Mohammed Ghanim al-Rumaihi, *Al-bitrol wa al-taqhayur al-ijtimai fi al-khalij al-arabi* [Oil and social change in the Arab gulf] (Kuwait: Muusasat al-Wihdah lil wa- al-Tawzi, 1975), *Muawiqat al-tanniyah al-ijtimaiyah wa- al-iqtisadiyah, fi mujtamaat al-khalij al-arabi al-muasirah* [Social and economic obstacles to development in the contemporary Arab gulf] (Kuwait: Kazhima, 1977), and *Al-khalij laysa naftan* [The gulf beyond oil] (Kuwait: Kazhima, 1983).

2   See Abo I. Baaklini, "Legislatures in the Gulf Area: The Experience of Kuwait: 1961-76," *International Journal of Middle East Studies* 14 (1982):359-379; and Ahmad J. Dhaher and Faisal Al-Salem, "Kuwait's Parliamentary Elections", *Journal of Arab Affairs* 3, no. 1:85-98. On the Cabinet, see Abdul-Reda Assiri and Kamal Al-Manoufi, *The Middle East Journal* 42, no. 1(Winter 1988): 48-58.

3   See Karl Deutsch, "Social Mobilization and Political Development", *American Political Science Review* 55 (September 1961); W. W. Rostow, *Politics and the Stages of Growth* (London: Cambridge University Press, 1971); Alex Inkeles and David Smith, *Becoming Modern: Individual Change in Six Developing Countries* (Cambridge: Harvard University Press, 1974); Daniel Lerner, *The Passing of Traditional Society: Modernizing the Middle East* (New York: The Free Press, 1958). See also Leonard Binder (ed.), *The Study of the Middle East* (New York: John Wiley and Sons, 1976), for a critique of this approach. See Tawfic E. Farah and Faisal Al-Salem, "The Traditionalism and Modernization Dichotomy: The Cases of Lebanon and Kuwait", *Journal of Social Sciences* 4 (April 1976): 38-52; D. C. Tipps, "Modernization Theory and the Comparative Study of Societies: A Critical Perspective", *Comparative Studies in Society and History* 15 (1973); J. R. Gusfield, "Tradition and Modernity: Misplaced Polarities in the Study of Social Change", *American Journal of Society* 72 (1967); M. Kesselman, "Order or Movement: The Literature of Political Development as Ideology", *World Politics* 26 (1973); Samuel Huntington, "The Change to Change: Modernization, Development and Politics", *Comparative Politics* 3 (April 1971). For reviews of this literature, see R. A. Packenham, *Liberal America and the Third World* (Princeton, N.J.: Princeton University Press, 1973); Samuel Huntington and Jorge Dominguez, "Political Development", in *Macro Political Theory: 3, Handbook of Political Science*, Fred Greenstein and Nelson Polsyby (eds.) (Reading, Mass.: Addison Wesley, 1975); Richard Higgott, "From Modernization Theory to Public Policy: Continuity and Change in the Political Science of Political Development", *Studies in Comparative International Development* 15 (1980).

4   See F. H. Cardoso and E. Faletto, *Dependency and Development in Latin American* (Berkeley: University of California Press, 1979); Andre Gundar Frank, *Capitalism and Underdevelopment in Latin America* (New York: Monthly Review Press, 1967). In this general vein flow also the word systems approaches, e.g., Immanuel Wallerstein, *The Modern World System* (New York: Academic Press, 1974). While this grew out of Latin American studies, it had its Middle Eastern contributors, notably Samir Amin, *The Arab Nation* (London: Zed Press, 1976); *Accumulation on a World Scale* (London: Monthly Review Press, 1974); Jacqueline Ismael, *Kuwait: Social Change in Historical Perspective* (Syracuse: Syracuse University Press, 1982).

5   For a compendium of political culture studies in Kuwaiti and Gulf contexts, see Tawfic E. Farah (ed.), *Political Behavior in the Arab States* (Boulder, C.O.: Westview Press, 1983); Farah and Yasumasa Kuroda (eds.), *Political Socialization in the Arab States* (Boulder, C.O.: Lynne Reinner Inc., 1987). For a refreshing look at Arab political culture, see also Hisham Sharabi, *Neopatriarchy: A Theory of Distorted Change in Arab Society* (New York: Oxford University Press, 1988).

6   Hazem Beblawi and Giacomo Luciani (eds.), *The Rentier State* (London: Croom Helm, 1987).

7   N. Mahdavy, "The Patterns and Problems of Economic Development in Rentier States: The Case of Iran", in *Studies in the Economic History of the Middle East*, M. A. Cook (ed.), (London: Oxford University Press, 1970), pp. 428-9.

8   Some examples of ruling family involvement in the private sector are now more readily found. For example, the case of Nasir Sabah al-Ahmad al-Sabah, son of the foreign minister and nephew of the Emir, who is chairman of United Realty, United Fisheries, Gulf International, and the Sharja Group.

9   See Ahmad J. Dhaher, *Al-biroqiratiya fi al-khalij* [Bureaucracy in the gulf] (Kuwait: Dhat Al Salasil, 1984), and Ahmad J. Dhaher and Faisal Al-Salem, *Al-amala fi duwal al-khalij al-arabi* [Expatriate labor in the gulf] (Kuwait: Dhat al Salasil, n.d.).

10   Tawfic E. Farah and Faisal Al-Salem, "Political Efficacy, Political Trust, and the Action Orientation of University Students in Kuwait", *International Journal of Middle East Studies* 8 1977):317-28.

11   Charles Telly (ed.), *The Formation of National States in Western Europe* (Princeton, N.J.: Princeton University Press, 1975), and Yousef Cohen, Brian Brown, and Aifik Organski, "The Paradoxical Nature of State Making: The Violent Creation of Order", *American Political Science Review* 75 (1981).

12   Robert Springborg, "On the Rise and Fall of Arab Isms", *Australian Outlook* 31(1):92-109.

13   Bernard Lewis, "Loyalties to Community, Nation and State", in G. S. Wise and C. Isawi (eds.), *Middle East Perspectives: The Next Twenty Years* (Princeton, N.J.: Darwin Press, 1981).

Development and the State in Post-Colonial Algeria

RACHID TLEMCANI

University of Algiers, Algiers, Algeria

AND

WILLIAM W. HANSEN

University of Maryland, College Park, MD, U.S.A.

ABSTRACT

This article analyses the role of Algerian bureaucracy in development. It shows that the Algerian state owns the significant means of production and has used the bureaucracy to implement its statist model of development. In doing so it has emphasized the development of heavy industry and the use of the most advanced technology available to promote it. It was hoped that with this model of development and the help of a skilled and trained bureaucracy, rapid industrial growth would transform the country's socio-economic structure sufficiently to absorb the masses of peasant labour and allow Algeria to produce anything it chooses. This model, however, failed to create jobs for the bulk of the Algerian population, led to heavy reliance on foreign capital, and created large pools of unemployed and under-employed. For two decades these problems were staved off when high oil prices shaped the relationship between bureaucracy and development. When oil prices went down drastically in the 1980s, they caused unrest and turmoil in Algeria and created an economic crisis which the State and its bureaucracy are currently trying to manage.

I. Introduction: Some Theoretical Considerations

Radicals over the last thirty years have been concerned with developing a comprehensive theory of the state in its multiplicitous forms: capitalist, socialist (communist), and postcolonial. The first two will not concern us here except to provide an occasional comparison between the postcolonial state and those of Eastern Europe also dominated (ruled) by privileged, exploiting bureaucratic classes. With regard to the postcolonial state, these analysts have been interested in explaining why this bureaucratic state class has played a more central role in social change than an indigenous entrepreneurial bourgeoisie. Algeria is a society in which the state, dominated by a political-bureaucratic class, owns the significant means of production while it controls and determines virtually all productive investment, most of which has gone into rapid and dependent industrialization.

The first writer to develop an explicit theory of the postcolonial state was Hamza Alavi[1]. Briefly Alavi attributes the nature of this type of social formation to structural changes brought about by colonialism and the superstructural institutions consequent upon them. This is further affected, then, by the radical realignment of class forces upon independence: metropolitan capital, the indigenous (nationalist) aspirant bourgeoisie, and the landed classes. The indigenous bourgeoisie, however, is "weak and underdeveloped" and thus unable to "subordinate" the colonial state apparatus it has been bequeathed. The three exploiting classes on the morrow of independence now have competing but no longer antagonistic interests. A bureaucracy-military elite thus takes charge of the state to mediate these "competing" but not "contradictory" demands. The state acquires "a relatively autonomous role and is not simply the instrument of any one of these classes"[2].

Much of Alavi's argument is relevant to the Algerian case. There are, however, some problems and they relate to the overdeveloped apparatus: bureaucracy, military oligarchy, relative autonomy, coalition, dominant class, etc. The bureaucracy, according to Alavi and other writers on the postcolonial state, does not constitute a new class but merely mediates between existing ones[3]. It is our assertion that in Algeria the state bureaucratic bourgeoisie has indeed itself become a class[4]. It organizes the labor process and the distribution of surplus value. It controls and determines the nature of investment and the process of capital accumulation. It reproduces itself through nepotism and corruption as well as by control over access to cultural capital, i.e., higher education and the acquisition of technical skills. This complete task can only be accomplished because the state bureaucracy has monopolized and appropriated the oil rent and that of other mineral resources. This monopolization is the basis of its power.

There is no sector of the reproduction of social life where the state does not intervene directly or indirectly. Its acts as lawmaker, investor, planner, importer, exporter, manager, owner, judge, and police officer. The state in postcolonial Algerian society—and the bureaucratic class that "owns" it—is everything. In the Arab world "political society", in the Gramscian sense, predominates over "civil society" which is still at an embryonic stage.

II. Historical Stages of State Formation

In order to understand the roots of the present Algerian state, it is instructive to take a brief look at the country's history and how it helped to shape political structures. In Algerian history one might postulate four stages in the formation of the state:

1) Under Ottoman rule (1519-1830) Algeria was governed by a "semi-feudal" state. State/society was marked by military coercion. The Ottoman bureaucracy was more attached to economic plunder than to the Western principle of profitability; that is to say it was not guided by a Weberian "spirit of capitalism".

2) French colonial rule (1830-1962) profoundly disrupted the pre-existing order. However, instead of introducing the supposed benefits of the bourgeois

revolution, it is intituted an absolutist military-bureaucratic regime, the consequence of which was an extremely uneven, distorted, and dependent development that included the massive and systematic dispossession of the peasantry and the working masses in general[5].

3) The third stage saw the rise of an Algerian ''petty bourgeoisie'' at the onset of the twentieth century. Denied full access to the accumulation process, this intelligentsia became increasingly nationalist and anti-colonial while assuming control of the opposition movement—ultimately the FLN (Front de la Libération Nationale). Although the intelligentsia leadership, the peasantry, and the small but growing working class have a common colonial enemy at the outset of the struggle, their interests eventually diverge; for the intelligentsia the construction of a strong, centralized state; for the peasantry and working class land reform, cooperative enterprises, and distributive justice.

4) The fourth stage saw the assumption of control by the nationalist leadership in the postcolonial period. This was marked by the rapid transformation of the bureaucratic military elite into a new class. Organized politically through a fractious war, the new state class ''renovated'' but did not fundamentally alter, the colonial apparatus. In this manner the obstacles that had previously inhibited its political and economic emancipation were destroyed and the state itself was turned into its vehicle of accumulation.

III. Revolutionary Populism and Transition to State Power

The period immediately after the end of the war of independence was the point at which the aspirant state bourgeoisie was the weakest. The Algerian people as a whole were highly mobilized and flushed with the euphoria of victory over French colonialism. To a significant degree the masses had absorbed the wartime revolutionary rhetoric of socialism, equality, democracy, progress, prosperity, and workers' control. At the same time the political elite was riven with internal conflict.

Independence was accompanied by the mass flight of European settlers. Although ''just'' compensation was provided for in the Evian Agreement many of the settlers sold cars, villas, cafes, land, business, and factories at ridiculously low prices. Others simply abandoned their properties and fled in panic to wait in Europe for a return to political stability. Some well-off Algerians followed the latter to Europe ''to look for repatriates willing to sell them their farms, their businesses, their factories. By this stalling for the property titles, the Algerian bourgeoisie set about inheriting French colonization''[6]. Leading members of the state apparatus also rushed individually to seize abandoned properties. In all these instances it was well connected and wealthy Algerians who were able to profit from settler flight.

However, the masses also responded to this ''revolutionary opportunity'' and began spontaneously to occupy *collectively* some of the abandoned land and factories. The UGTA (Union Générale des Travailleurs Algériens) supported this occupation and assisted the organization of self-management committees.

The result was that some 1.2 million hectares of fertile land and 1,000 industrial and commercial units were occupied. This spontaneous mass action constituted a fundamental threat to the bureaucratic state elite's notion of revolution from the top down under complete state control. This new oligarchy in attempting to consolidate its power was faced with the choice of either institutionalizing the spontaneous collective occupations and self-management or confronting the masses directly with force. The latter course, because of the state class' relative weakness and lack of consolidation at the time, was impossible. The consequence was the March Decrees (1963) in which self-management was juridically recognized but placed gradually under the tutelage of a conservative state bureaucracy which proceeded to de-radicalize the entire movement.

In retrospect it seems clear that this period of spontaneous mass action was truly a revolutionary one. Also in retrospect it seems virtually inevitable that it would be crushed. The external and internal forces arrayed against it were so formidable as to seem overwhelming. These forces were aided by the political, cultural, and organizational immaturity of the masses who carried out the occupations.

Those supporting a bureaucratic, centralized version of self-management argued that these production units were too weak to succeed by themselves. Consequently, they needed to be incorporated into the national production plan and given the managerial guidance they required. A transitional stage would have to be undergone in which both the revolutionary state and the self-management phenomenon would consolidate their strength. The bureaucratic agency created for this task in the agricultural sector was the National Office of Agrarian Reform (ONRA). ONRA was seen as a neutral agency mediating between the self-managed production units and the state. In fact it was merely a fusion of several colonial agencies which had in the past oppressed the masses. Its theoretical justification was that it functioned "to find the right mean between the anarchist workerist tendency of the base and the centralizing, bureaucratic, statist current at the top"[7]. ONRA was given authority over the self-management committees which vitiated the meaning of the term. Responsibility for sales on the internal as well as world market were turned over to state agencies that were part of ONRA. Accounting transactions and seed distribution were determined by them. Most of the middle level bureaucrats in these agencies had been employed by the colonial state in the same positions. The state also controlled all financing of long- and short-term loans to the self-managed sector, which crippled their capacity to remain independent. Finally ONRA and local FLN units manipulated the elections so as to control local self-management leadership committees.

A similar mechanism was used to take over factory councils. Many local committees were dissolved in the name of efficiency, productivity, and profitability. By the end of 1963 industrial, artisanal, and mining self-management committees were placed under the control of the Economics Ministry.

IV. The Bureaucratic State: Consolidation of Power and Development Policy

By the time of Houari Boumedienne's 1965 coup the process of demobilizing the masses had been largely completed, as had the process of consolidation on the part of the bureaucratic bourgeoisie. This enabled the new state class to begin full implementation of its statist model of accumulation.

The exact development implemented was largely of Western European provenance[8]. In short it called for an emphasis on heavy industry using the most advanced technology available. Investment would be concentrated in "industrializing industries"; i.e., industries that would function as "poles of growth" and stimulate other secondary and tertiary industrial growth. In Algeria these poles of heavy industry were to be primarily hydrocarbons and metallurgy from which chemicals, machine tools, building materials, and electronics would develop.

According to this development model, by the early 1980s rapid industrial growth would have transformed the socio-economic structure sufficiently to absorb the mass of peasant labor and allow Algeria to produce virtually anything it chose. This model, of course, has a resonance to that pursued by the Soviet Union under both Lenin, who was also fascinated by a state-owned "Taylorism"[9], and Stalin, who carried the model to its extreme during the thirties. While the Soviet experience may have resulted in rapid industrial growth it hardly produced socialism, the goal for which the Soviet working class was struggling, presumably, during the October Revolution.

In terms of the Algerian model it was argued that a deepening of the domestic market required a substantial increase in GNP that could be brought about only through an enormous increase in labor productivity. The most sophisticated technology was required to accomplish this end. The "industrializing" industries—so-called economic locomotives—would adequately supply agriculture with the necessary inputs allowing it to increase its product. Industrial and agricultural growth would then supply the mass of population with food, consumer goods, as well as capital goods. Because the landed classes would resist the "technical revolution" in the countryside there must be a thorough-going land reform. The underlying premise is that authoritarianism is a necessary condition for rural development.

To summarize: Technically advanced heavy industry must take precedence over employment, consumption, housing, and agricultural development as these are all independent upon it. In the jargon of Western (and Eastern) modernization theory there is a conflict between economic growth and political participation[10]. The political elite has no choice but to favor rapid economic growth to the detriment of both socio-economic equality and political participation during the period of initial accumulation and take off.

One of the main problems with this model, however, is that it fails to create jobs for the bulk of the population. As well, it tends to favor the urban middle classes and skilled workers while creating vast pools of un- and under-employment. (A mere glance at modern Algiers will show large numbers of unemployed young men standing around on every street corner). The advocates of this development model regard advanced technology as being politically and socially neutral. On the contrary, it is impregnated with the values and practices of the societies in which it originated and brings with it those very same structural relationship: a basically capitalist and alienated work process.

One wonders often whether, in fact, Algeria even has a coherent state plan. Not only have the externally oriented sectors received the bulk of planned investments—an anticipated reality—but actual investments in these sectors have generally exceeded these amounts. For example, in the first three plans (1967-1978) actual investment in the petroleum sector exceeded the planned amount by significant margins each time, During the same period, investments in the domestically oriented sectors of agriculture and infrastructure—sectors that would benefit large numbers of Algerians themselves—was often significantly less than planned[11].

Up to this point we have discussed only the accumulation process as carried out by large state-owned enterprises occupying the leading sectors of the Algerian political economy. However, the private sector—deeply articulated with the state sector—is not unimportant and has been growing. Although private ownership of the means of production was never prohibited by either the "Marxist" Tripoli Program or the Algiers Charter, the 1976 Constitution refers to some forms of private capital as being compatible with "Algerian socialism"[12]. However, there is little reliable data on the private sector, a paucity that leads one to speculate as to the relations between it and the state bourgeoisie[13]. Many private companies are owned *de facto* by members of the state bourgeoisie, although *de jure* by their families and friends. Small-scale private capital exists in metal production and processing, chemicals, rubber food processing, textiles and clothing, leather and shoes, wood processing and paper, and construction. These are labeled "non-exploitative" private capital, confusing their sectoral occurrence with relations of production. The private sector is concentrated in consumer products oriented to short-term realization of surplus value using inputs purchased from the state sector.

What is apparent is that the private sector has been growing steadily and assuming an increasingly important role in Algerian life. In the 1977 census it was disclosed that the private sector employs 52.6 percent of those employed in construction; 45.3 percent in chemicals and plastics; and 35 percent in wood processing[14]. In 1982 in accounted for 40 percent in transportation, 70 percent in agriculture, and 75 percent of all employment in commerce. By 1983 more than one-third of the national labor force was employed by the private sector. A 1982 report by the US Embassy in Algiers reported the existence of 315,000 private enterprises[15]. Obviously the vast bulk of these are micro-enterprises, but a significant proportion of their production seems to be relative luxury goods (carpets, furniture, construction of private villas, other gadgets) intended for a particular social stratum.

As mentioned earlier, private production is concentrated in downstream activities with inputs from the highly capitalized state sector. The inputs from these industries are transferred at a low cost to the private sector which transforms and then valorizes them in a de-regulated domestic market almost totally controlled by private capital. Often these inputs are transferred at less than their cost which means that the profits realized in the private sector are a by-product of the devalorization of the public sector[16]. Furthermore, there is the over-exploitation of the private sector workforce through lower wages and regressive working conditions[17].

Although the question of land reform has been an integral part of the nationalist discourse from the beginning, virtually no redistribution had taken place in the liberated areas during the war and for the first ten years of independence. That which eventually did take place can be understood, from the point of view of the state bourgeoisie, as having two purposes: first, it was an attempt to neutralize the peasantry politically as a source of opposition and, secondly, to recruit them as allies in the bureaucracy's struggle against the agrarian bourgeoisie and absentee landlords. Economically it aimed at more fully incorporating the rural economy into the national market so as partly to help finance the urban oriented accumulation process.

Despite the socialist rhetorical flourishes surrounding the announcement of the Charter of the Agrarian Revolution[18], in 1971 agrarian reform basically functioned as a mechanism of surplus drainage from the rural to the urban areas. Although mechanisms for peasant participation in the various agrarian reform institutional structures were created these remained largely a facade[19]. As with nearly all other institutional structures in Algeria, the centralized bureaucratic state apparatus controlled virtually all aspects of it. The lands assigned to the agrarian revolution were relatively poor and the supposed beneficiaries, the landless and smallholding peasants, had no voice in the land allotments. The administrative leadership of the cooperatives was appointed by the centralized state, not chosen by the members.

A new land reform law was implemented in the 1980-84 period which aimed essentially are restructuring the state agricultural sector. Selfmanaged units and "Agrarian Revolution" co-ops became unified as the *Domaines Agricoles Socialistes* (DAS) of which 3,364 were created. The remaining plots of land were de-nationalized and distributed to individual ownership[20].

In December 1987 still another law was promulgated, the purpose of which was to break up the DAS units into *Exploitations Agricoles Collectives* (EAC). By the middle of April, 1988, a total of 12,108 EAC units had been created, each made up of seven persons[21]. An additional 1,462 one-person unites of private property were created. When the 1987 law becomes fully implemented in the near future, the number of private landholdings will increase dramatically. It is needless to point out that most of these individual holdings have been and will continue to be appropriated by members of the state ruling class.

V. Algeria and the World Economy

In the past, Algeria has often been perceived in both East and West as a "radical" Arab state. Its development strategy for a quarter century has made it almost a prototypical example of what is referred to in the Soviet Union and the East Bloc as the "non-capitalist road"[22]. However, radical socialist rhetoric notwithstanding, the history of independent Algeria has witnessed a consistent deepening of its relationship to and dominance by international capitalism.

Algerian development has been largely financed by international capital. Borrowing on the international capital markets and various other industrial development schemes have not been for one-time purposes but, in fact, have become an integral part of the way in which the Algerian state has financed its entire operation. Increasingly MNCs take out more in annual profits from third world countries than they re-invest, producing a "capital drain", i.e., most new investments are financed by locally generated profits.

While Algerian debt may seem minor compared states such as Mexico, Brazil, and Argentina, it is among the highest in the Arab world. The so-called "industrializing industries" (petro-chemicals and metallurgy) have been almost completely financed by international capital[23]. Although Algeria may still maintain its "radical" image to the world at large, by the mid-seventies Western bankers knew differently, i.e., there were healthy profits to be made in Algeria through dealing with a very cooperative state[24].

Tensions with France in the early seventies with regard to the 1965 Franco-Algerian immigrant workers in France, led to a strong re-orientation of Algerian policy toward the United States. Oil and gas outlets were opened up to American companies and important delivery contracts were signed with Commonwealth, Exxon, Gulf, and Sun Oil companies in 1972[25]. By 1980 the United States was purchasing more than half of all Algerian petroleum exports. The U.S. also became dominant in the sphere of providing loans and various consultation services.

The "logical" ally of radical Algeria according to the theory of the non-capitalist road, the Soviet Union, and the East European OMEA, was dominant only in mining and military assistance and since 1980 Algeria has been trying to limit the latter reliance. One estimate had the Algerian arms market as worth a potential US $3 billion during the latter part of the eighties[26]. At the end of President Chadli Benjedid's visit to the US in April, 1985, Ronald Reagan characterized Algeria as a "friendly country".

The vast majority of all Algerian contracts for the installation of new industrial plant and equipment have been done through tenders in which foreign engineering companies take responsibility for implementation. There are two implicit assumptions contained in this relationship with foreign firms:
1) economic development based on technology transfer is less expensive in the long run; and
2) sophisticated technology will stimulate national development to the extent that it will generate its own technology in the future[27].

This theory of economic development is accepted both by traditional theorists as well as by those advocating a New International Economic Order (NIEO). The last thirty years, however, have shown this to be a delusion. The reality has been a financial plunder of the third world and distorted development—Algeria included. Engineering firms typically are involved in two phases of so-called technology transfer:

1) engineering studies concerning marketing research, investment profitability, equipment assembly, and technological adaptation; and

2) social relations in the workplace such as unit organization and management, construction, supervision, and personnel training.

During Algeria's first four-year plan nearly two-thirds of all new industrial units were so-called "turnkey" plants. Thus choices involving equipment, licenses, and manufacturing methods are the foreign contractor's responsibility. This new technology is hardly socially neutral. It contains what are fundamentally capitalist, ie., exploitative and alienated, relations of production. This applies also to projects carried out in cooperation with OMEA countries as well as the West[28].

In Algeria the workers' councils called for a radical generalization of self-management in these turnkey plants but the imported technology, impregnated with the power relationship of its source, tends ineluctably to fragment the working class and undermine self-management and any attempt to create truly socialist relations of production. The foreign engineering firms and their resulting product become capitalist enclaves and realize extraordinary profits: investment fees, over-invoicing, very high cost for "expert" consulting services, management advisory services, etc. From 1973 to 1978 the portion of technical assistance as a part of the total cost of these contracts averaged 36.2 percent[29].

While Algeria may have diversified its customers somewhat in terms of external trade, it is very restricted as to the source from which it can purchase technology. Often a single technological innovation dominates the entire world market and is monopolized by a very few firms. The problems of technology transfer are exacerbated by the absence of an institutional capacity in third world countries to reproduce it. Thus they have little actual control over:

1) the type of technology to be imported,

2) the adaptation of it to fit national realities, and

3) the linkages of the selected technology, both internally and internationally.

In the Algerian case technology transfer has widened the gap between the propertied and laboring classes.

A coherent approach to this problem would consist of controlling and coordinating its transfer while simultaneously promoting an institutional capacity in the third world. However, it is doubtful as to whether the peripheral state even has this option. Given the existing international division of labor, one notes that 98 percent of all research and development facilities, trained manpower (even if they are of third world origins and/or nationality), organizational skills, etc. necessary to embark on innovation are concentrated in the developed countries. Furthermore, the above does not deal with the whole question of patents. Licensing agreements and contracts are laden with restrictions which prevent the third world from producing its own technology[30].

The bureaucratic phenomenon has become so powerful in Algeria that even some leading figures in the state power bloc have felt compelled to criticize it. The new National Charter devoted several pages to the negative aspects of bureaucratic paralysis[31]. However, from the point of view of the hegemonic political bloc an attack on bureaucratic inefficiency can only be from the top down; thus what is required is a "solid and ever strengthened state"[32]. This, of course, is what engendered the bureaucratic phenomenon in the first place.

In spite of the official recognition that bureaucracy functions as a constraint on economic development and social change the power block assumes that the rational-legal bureaucracy that it is trying to create has a special virtue and will be able to supervise anti-bureaucratic measures:

> It is the responsibility of the authorities at every level to search out and set in motion adequate solutions that will hold or bring back the administrative structures to their proper role of supporting production and running the country's affairs smoothly[33].

This is a classic example of hiring the fox to guard the henhouse. The state never intends to allow really independent institutions with actual political power that would be able to bring significant pressure for change in existing bureaucratic institutions.

Anti-bureaucratic campaigns are not unusual in post-colonial states. Nor, for that matter, are they non-existent in more economically advanced states. U.S. presidents Jimmy Carter and Ronald Reagan were elected largely by campaigning against the national bureaucracy. Mikhail Gorbachev, the General-Secretary of the CPSU, has made a virtual industry out of an anti-bureaucratic struggle. This phenomenon has been most often simply a method of establishing political legitimacy by rhetorical flourishes aimed at quieting a restive population. Blaming "faceless" bureaucrats for the problem encountered by the people is a widely used technique.

In Algeria there has been a seeming wave of anti-bureaucratic actions including the trials of former Foreign Minister Abdelaziz Bouteflika and other high level figures on charges of corruption. In the post-colonial state there are three interrelated reasons for these anti-bureaucratic campaigns:
1) the new "Prince" must eliminate the predecessor's clique;
2) excessive dissipation of the social surplus prejudices accumulation and the subsequent reproduction of the bureaucratic bourgeoisie itself;
3) the anti-bureaucratic movement legitimates the new regime[34].

There is some sort of commission of inquiry in virtually every third world country. Corruption, as James Scott points out, is a cement that holds together a conservative social bloc[35]. In Algeria each state corporation was set up to engage in a specific economic sector, but their operational criteria were not rigorously defined. Their sphere of activities rapidly expanded. Since each firm is responsible for its own productivity and profitability, they began to compete with each other in the national market. The control of the central political power over state corporations is very loose. In the early period a state enterprise was tolerated even if it failed to make a substantial profit. Until the establishment of the Audit Court (1978) the state's financial control over public enterprises barely existed. Many firms became not only economically, but also politically powerful. This often resulted in them being able to defy even the wishes of the state's top economic planners[36].

VI. Impending Crisis and Attempts at Reform

According to the economic reforms of the early eighties, major state corporations were forced to give up activities not directly connected to their sectoral specialization. The implicit core of the state's argument was that the deficits of the state firms were caused by their autonomy from state control. By breaking these monopolistic giants up the locus of economic decisions would be dispersed, making them more easily managed politically and economically by the Ministry of Planning[37]. Sonatrach, the state oil firm which formerly employed 100,000 people, was broken into thirteen separate units. Sonocome, concerned with vehicles, was broken into six units. In addition to administrative reforms, credits became more freely available and the establishment of more joint ventures was encouraged. Strict profitability considerations became required. The economic liberalization was referred to as market socialism by the Vice-Minister of Commerce[38]. The process of breaking up giant state corporations reached a turning point with new legislation in January, 1988. The new law (88.01 January 12, 1988) accords autonomous power to managers to run their firms strictly according to the law of profit.

Until this point the state bourgeoisie has resisted the adoption of free market laws on the Western model as advocated by the IMF. They are simply not in the best interest of that class at the present time. Among other things they would negate the state bourgeoisie's reason for existing. However, as James Petras has noted, the free enterprise system may be on the long term agenda. As some state firms become profitable and a wealthy private sector develops with ties to the top executives of the public companies, there will be pressure to privatize the profitable ones and allow the less profitable ones to remain under state ownership[37]. A January 1988 law, aimed at reorganizing the management of public sector corporations which had been broken up in the early eighties, emphasizes this trend. Managers will form their own financial base and, more importantly, a system of share certificates has been set up which will give impetus to the ultimate privatization of the public sector.

Uneven income distribution inevitably follows the political choice calling for rapid industrialization and the subsequent austerity policy is borne almost completely by the lower classes. Wage disparity in Algeria exceeded 20 to 1 in the eighties when one considers, in addition to official wage disparities, all the bonuses and the in-kind perquisites available to the upper class: high executives of central and local administrations, upper army officers, and managers of various economic units in Eastern European terminology—the nomenklatura. This latter *de facto* income is largely devoted to luxury items such as cars, villas, maids, chauffeurs, special gifts, and generally unavailable low-priced consumer goods. These managers, officers, and high officials are able to appropriate a large fraction of the social surplus and, as in this way, constitute an exploitative class.

Because of the entire development strategy from the beginning (expensive imported technology) the cost of creating new jobs has been very high. In 1977 it was estimated that it cost nearly a half million dinars to create a single job in the petrochemical or metallurgical industries[40]. According to official figures the unemployment rate declined between 1967 and 1977, from over 30 percent to slightly over 20 percent. However, even if accepted at face value—a dubious assertion, at best—these figures do not reflect the social reality. They exclude from the category "active population" all those between 15 and 18 years of age (then 7 percent of the population) and from 59-65 (then 3%)[41] Furthermore, the half million emigrants in Europe are excluded. The actual rate had to be higher than one-third of the total labor force. If one includes women, who are virtually ignored by official data, it can be inferred that state policy has marginalized about two-thirds of the total work force[42]. Under the recently imposed austerity program, the urban unemployment rate has reached forty percent, producing a potentially explosive situation.

Not only has Algeria created too few jobs, but the ones it has created have overwhelmingly been white collar jobs, this in a society that is still basically rural. Naturally, at independence the state "Algerianized" the administrative apparatus. This was also a fundamental first step in the creation of a new class. A 1982 estimate indicated that about one-third of the national budget was being spent annually on education, clearly a technical requisite of industrialization[43]. Between 1963-1980 the Algeria university system trained nearly 32,000 graduates. In the 1980-84 period another 43,000 were graduated[44]. During the 1987-88 academic year nearly 200,000 students were enrolled in Algerian universities. Until recently the state guaranteed university graduates a job making the intelligentsia, *prima facie*, an ally of the regime. However, the current crisis has radically changed this situation. Many graduates, even some with advanced degrees, are unable to find the kind of position that heretofore has been considered their right.

Underdevelopment is often explained in terms of lack of trained personnel. For Algeria this is hardly the case. First of all, the public administration and economic sectors are heavily overstaffed with the consequent underutilization of large numbers of trained personnel. Secondly, one must consider the large number of skilled Algerians who live abroad. At least one-third of all native Algerian physicians in the '70s live in Europe. Approximately one-fifth of all Algerian skilled workers live in Europe, primarily France. Algerian planning strategists have long been well aware of this[45]. It seems an ironic contradiction that a poor, underdeveloped country, in need of trained manpower, finds itself unable to utilize that which it has.

What Algeria lacks, then, is not trained personnel, but a coherent, coordinate strategy with regard to educational development. There is no real attempt to stem the steady brain drain. In fact, one could argue that the state might be encouraging it as a mechanism for skimming off a significant fraction of the population that might otherwise contribute significantly to political instability, i.e., give a coherent leadership to the marginalized and unemployed[46].

Considering constant shortages, unemployment, high inflation, the housing crisis, etc. it is clear that the living conditions of the laboring classes have declined precipitously. Furthermore, there has been a state policy of "cleaning up" some urban areas. In the coastal cities random identity checks arte a routine part of daily life. Since 1982 demolition of urban slums has only exacerbated the housing crises. Over a million slum dwellers in Oran, Constantine, and Algiers have been uprooted and sent back to their native villages. When this same policy of "influx control" and "forced relocation" is carried out by the white regime in South Africa, the Algerian government vigorously (and correctly) denounces it. In Algeria it is considered legitimate state policy. Presumably it is fundamentally different when it is done by whites than when one's "own kind" brutalizes the vulnerable and helpless.

VII. Response and Resistance from Below

In the early sixties the more horizontally structured (i.e. not overly centralized) local unions played an important part in political education and most of the strikes in that period were decided upon locally with limited central interference. In many cases the workers forced the state to nationalize the factories they had taken over from notoriously oppressive settlers[47]. However, this spontaneous popular activism was not welcomed by the new "socialist" state and the FLN Party saw the decentralized structure of the UGTA as a possible framework from which direct workers' control might emerge in the future. This conflict between the UGTA and the FLN led to an anti-union offensive[48]. This offensive had begun at the UGTA's first congress in 1963 and continued for the next several years. In 1967, for example, striking oil workers were summarily fired causinf the UGTA's organ, *Révolution et Travail*, to criticize "neobourgeois" elements who do not hesitate to fire activists and elected representatives of the workers[49].

The consequences led to a threat by the UGTA in 1967 to call a general strike, but the moderate wing of the federation prevailed arguing that a strike was not proper in a time of economic difficulties. In the aftermath of an abortive left wing coup several months later, most of the revolutionary syndicalists were arrested and the state began to enforce vigorously its policy of organically integration the union movement into the party-state. Kaid Ahmed, the FLN-Party head, announced:

> a radical change in the syndicate's organic structures so as to avoid any sterile criticism in the future. We have decided to place all the national organizations under the direct authority of the *commissariat national de parti*... It is a good time to eliminate the harmful elements that have infiltrated in party and national organizations[50].

By the time the Third UGTA Congress was held, the FLN Party had already selected the delegates, repeating the tactics used at the First Congress in 1963. Heavily centralized vertical structures were installed and local autonomy was virtually ended. By 1969 the federation's own organ specified the UGTA's new role:

> The UGTA is the necessary and complementary partner of the party and must be contribute to the realization of the objectives of production, without any contestation[51].

The Party's paper, *El Moudjahid*, echoed this by arguing that the UGTA's role was to instill discipline and responsibility in the workers[52]. The Ministry of Labor argued that national development was impossible in a climate of conflict and tension, thus work stoppages must end[53].

The UGTA was thus transformed into a state appendage—a transmission belt between the administration and the working class. No longer could the union represent the interests of the workers as such. Instead it was to help enforce state decisions and the Ministry of Labor was the institution given charge of enforcing this policy. The interests of the state and those of the workers were seen as being indistinguishable[54]. The underlying assumption is that the state is a state of the whole people and the idea that there could be conflicts between workers and the state is absurd on its face. Striking in the state sector thus became punishable by law under the 1978 labor code[55].

However, all oppositional working class action was not terminated by the incorporation of the UGTA into the bureaucratic structure. Autonomous actions in opposition to UGTA recommendation became so critical in the form of rolling strikes that Boumedienne was forced to recognize it in a speech to the UGTA executive[56]. This oppositional struggle which has continued throughout the eighties can be put in two different but related categories. The first is organized collective action: demonstrations, strikes, petitions, etc. These have taken place with dockworkers, bakers, workers, vehicle assemblers, in the state dairy enterprise, and with textile workers. Between 1967 and 1980 the number of strikes in the state sector increased more than fifteen times[57]. In 1986, and again in the fall of 1988, spontaneous work stoppages to protest the government's austerity program and the debilitating effect of hyperinflation on living standards have taken place[58].

The second form in which this oppositional activity takes place are individual in character: sabotage, lateness, absenteeism, overuse of sick days, and insubordination. According to the managerial board of Sonelec (the state electric-electronic company) absenteeism had become a form of collective struggle similar to the strike.

While the nationalist "intermediary classes" have transformed themselves into a new class as they achieved political, economic, and most importantly, military control over civil society, they have been unable to achieve a position of hegemony in the Gramscian sense. The legitimacy of the ruling bloc is questioned constantly and it is kept in power ultimately by the threat of actual use of force. The "cultural cement" needed to bind together a fragmented society is absent in Algeria.

The recent rise of what is called "Islamic fundamentalism" is but an aspect of this. More than two decades of modernization and industrialization have disenchanted the overwhelming majority of the people. As Maxime Rodinson has observed, those who have benefitted from the new social processes have often moved "toward skepticism, religious liberalism, freedom of behavior... a vague deism, or even atheism". At the same time, however, the poor, who have not benefitted and who, in fact, often perceive themselves to be worse off than before become "more attached to Islam in its most rigidly traditional form..." In this way they "direct their anger and recrimination against the privileges of the rich and powerful[59].

The eighties have seen "independent" mosques financed by private benefactors and collections from the faithful mushroom across the country. They are built in any available space: garages, apartments, schools, factories, hospitals, and shanty-towns. In addition there are over 5,000 state mosques in Algeria. It is ahistorical, however, to think this religious revival will ever push society back to some sort of theocratic dark age. It can only lead to a partial withdrawal of some achieved secularization, e.g., on the women's issue, or prevent further progressive measures. Basically the fundamentalists do not have a new development project of any kind. At least in the mercantalist sense they all believe in free enterprise.

In the 1980s the new social force having a heavy influence on state policies is made up of the youths[60], the unemployed, and the marginalized urban masses. In Algeria the industrial working class is not the focal point of social change as it was in 19th century Europe. This new force vehemently refuses to be manipulated and controlled by official populism, language, and myth, i.e., the politics of the petty bourgeosie that accompanied the national liberation struggle and post-independence "modernization". This radical, petty bourgeois rhetoric that overemphasizes the international struggle against imperialism to the detriment of the internal class struggle is no longer an effective tool for mass mobilization. This is particularly so with regard to the post-independence generation. It is from this social grouping that the fundamentalist movement is making rapid headway[61]. Feeling extremely alientated in a society that offers them virtually no economic, cultural, social, or political outlets, they are particularly vulnerable to psychologically and culturally based religious appeals. However, this group would be available to give themselves to any political movement that offered them an escape from their lives' idleness, boredom, and poverty. The reality, however, is that for more than a quarter century there has been no legal political outlet other than the ossified, authoritarian structures of the FLN Party. Given this reality it is to be expected that the masses of disaffected, unemployed, marginalized youth turn to the mosques and religious fundamentalism to give vent to their frustrations. The mosques are the only place in which this is legally possible. The mullahs, of course, are more than willing to exploit this opportunity.

VIII. Conclusion

Clearly, a systemic or organic crisis has been developing in Algeria for more than two decades. As has been shown in this article, the bureaucratic ruling elite has been aware of this impending crisis for some time, even if that class' grasp of its complexities has often been somewhat limited. The bureaucracy's awareness of this underlying instability is what accounts for its persistent, if spasmodic, attempts at reform. These attempts have always been half-hearted and insufficiently carried out because any thoroughgoing reform would have threatened the state class' always precarious purchase on stability.

The full onset of the crisis has been staved off for nearly fifteen years by the massive rise in oil prices during the seventies. Flush with petrodollars the state class literally went on a spending binge. Grandiose investment projects gave the illusion of prosperity and allowed the bureaucracy to maintain power. Awash in the returns on oil rent some of the proceeds inevitably trickled down to the working masses.

However, the eighties presented quite a different picture as oil prices began to decline—at first slowly but then precipitously. By 1986 this unexpected decline, along with the economic liberalization policies lauched earlier in the decade, reached a critical juncture. With the new land reform laws of 1987, in which what had earlier been called the "Agrarian Revolution" was effectively dismantled, the last symbol of the Algerian Revolution as an attempt to build a specific post-colonial socialist society was abandoned. One of the Third World's developmental success stories was rapidly disintegrating.

The fall in oil revenues immediately affected state policy in Algeria as it did in other oil exporting countries. Nigeria and Mexico are only two other conspicuous examples. Many social and economic projects were called off overnight and eliminated from Algeria's 1985-89 Plan. For the first time in the postcolonial period the state refers openly to a "reserve army" of unemployed in Algeria. Layoffs of thousands of workers have become commonplace[62]. The daily living conditions of the vast majority have suddenly and significantly worsened, while those of the wealthy minority have gotten even better. It is the welfare state in Algeria that is "withering away".

The oil rent, which produced over 95 percent of state revenues in 1984, has until now substantially shaped the relationship between bureaucracy and development, between politics and economy, between state and society. Recently, however, according to the official political-ideological discourse, the function of the state is to manage the "economic crisis". The state can no longer afford "generosity". The people are told, "It is time to get back to work".

The legitimacy of the state bureaucratic elite has been, since independence, deeply rooted in the social and political heritage of the armed struggle. Wit the rapid decline in oil income, the burden of sacrifice has shifted dramatically onto the shoulders of the marginalized majority. This, in turn, has caused the vast majority to begin seriously questioning the very legitimacy of the state itself.

Twenty-seven years ago Frantz Fanon wrote an essay entitled "The Pitfalls of National Consciousness"[63]. In it, with an irony only history can produce, Fanon outlined much of what became the political history of postcolonial Algeria. He attacked the national petty bourgeoisie, that very class that was to lead most of the Third World to independence. In an oblique way (a frontal attack at that time being impolitic) he warned his fellow revolutionaries against following in the footsteps of the 'statist' societies of Eastern Europe. He criticized "that famous dictatorship" deemed indispensable by its adherents which pretends to be with the people "but soon [is used] against them"[64].

In hindsight one must think he was warning his colleagues in the Algerian revolution, if not what to expect, at least what to guard against. Before the FLN even assumed power, Fanon would seem to have had an insight into the nature of its dominant elements. He argued that crude nationalism is but a mechanism for disguising the internal class struggle. The nationalist petty bourgeoisie had one desitre and that was to take the place of the colonialists, not to change society in a fundamental way. A single party would be used, he predicted, to maintain the fiction that the postcolonial state was a state of the whole people, thus making an attack upon ist hegemony an attack upon the nation—treason. In fact, he argued, the single party state"... is the modern form of the dictatorship of the [petty] bourgeoisie, unmasked, unpainted, unscrupulous, and cynical"[65].

As this essay was in its final typing, rioting, centered in the urban areas, particularly Algiers, broke out. The government has declared martial law and news reports speak of troops enforcing curfews and of shooting directly at demonstrators, leaving hundreds dead. As we have attempted to show in this paper, the current crisis comes as no surprise; it is the inevitable result of policies pursued by the Algerian state since its assumption of power in 1962. Even if the present unrest is put down and the state bureaucratic class maintains its unity (something which is by no means guaranteed) this will not be indicative of having arrived at anything more than a temporary hiatus. States requiring naked force to stay in power have a distinctly unstable future.

NOTES

1   Hamza Alavi, "The State in Post-Colonial Societies: Pakistan and Bangladesh", *New Left Review*, Nr. 74, 1972.

2   *Ibid.* For a full discussion of the relationship between the Third World state, local capital, and international capital with regard to Brazil see Peter Evans, *Dependent Development: The Alliance of Multinational, State, and Local Capital in Brazil*, Princeton, N.J.: Princeton University Press, 1979.

3   Marnia Lazreg, "Bureaucracy and Class: The Algerian Case Dialectic", *Dialectical Anthropology*, Vol. 4, 1976, p. 295.

4   Lenin defined class as follows: "We call classes large groups of people that are distinctive by the place they occupy in a definite historically established system of production; by their relations towards the means of production; by their role in the social system of labor; and consequently, by their method of obtaining the share of national wealth which they dispose of, and by the size of that share. Classes as such are groups of people one of which can appropirate the labor of another owing to the difference in their position in a given system of social economy". Cited in Tony Cliff, *State Capitalism in Russia*, London: Pluto Press, 1974, p. 166.

5   For a brief but rigorous analysis of colonial capitalism see S. Demia, "Pour une Analyse Critique du Nationalisme Algérien", *Revue Algérienne des Sciences Juridiques, Économiques, et Politiques*, Vol. XI, Nr. 4, 1974.

6   Sur la phase actuelle de la lutte des classes an Algérie". *Document Marxiste* as cited by Serge Koulytchizky in *L'autogestion, l'homme et l'état. L'expérience Algérienne*, Paris: Mouton, 1974.

7   Statement by Economics Minister B. Boumaza, cited in Ian Clegg, *Workers' Self-Management in Algeria*, New York: Monthly Revies Press, 1971, p. 66.

8   J. Paelynck, *La théorie du développement régional polarisé*, Cahiers, ISEA, March 1965. See also the work of Destane de Bernis which was geared specifically to the Algerian situation. De Bernis's model is elaborated in "Les industries industrialisantes et l'intégration économique régionale", *Archives d'ISEA*, Nr. 1, Vol. XXI, 1968. See also his "Les industries industrialisantes et les options Algériennes", *Revue Tiers Monde*, Nr. 47, 1971. For a critique of this model see W. Andreff and A. Hayab, "Les priorités industrielles de la planification Algérienne sont-elles vraiment industrialisantes", *Revue Tiers Monde*, Vol. XIX, Nr. 76, 1978.

9   "We must organize in Russia the study and teaching of the Taylor system and systematically try it out and adopt it to our own ends". V. I. Lenin, "The Immediate Tasks of the Soviet Government" in: *Lenin Selected Works*, Vol. II, Moscow: Progress Publishers, 1970, p. 663.

10 Samuel P. Huntington and James Nelson, *No Easy Choice. Political Participation in Developing Countries*, Cambridge, MA: Harvard University Press, 1976. This same point is persuasively made with regard to the Soviet Union in Philip Corrigan, Harvie Ramsay, Derek Sayer, *Socialist Construction and Marxist Theory: Bolshevism and its Critique*, New York: Monthly Review Press, 1978, particular chapters 2 and 3.

11 Abdellatif Benachenhou, *Planification et développement en Algérie, 1962-1980*. Algiers: Imprimerie Commerciale, 1980, p. 49.

12 The Tripoli Program (1962) and the Algiers Charter (1964) were policy programs adopted by the FLN that were considered at the time to be victories for the Party's "Marxist" wing. For an elaboration see Rachid Tlemcani, *State and Revolution in Algerie*, London: Zed Press, 1986, pp. 74 and 93.

13 Djillali Liabes, "Sur la bourgeoisie privée", *Les Temps Modernes*, Nrs. 432-433, p. 111 and B. Elsenhans, "Contradictions", *Maghreb Review*, Vol. 7, Nrs. 3, 4, 1984, p. 65.

14 Benachenhou, *op. cit.*, p. 98.

15 *Economist Intelligence Unit*, 1973, Nr. 3, p. 7.

16 *Maghreb Review, op. cit.*, p. 65.

17 For the description of private sector working conditions, see B. Semmoud, *Canadian Journal of African Studies*, Vol. 16, Nr. 2, 1982, p. 286.

18 On November 8, 1971 Col. Boumedienne referred to the land reform program as the second stage in the Algerian revolution; the first being the war for independence. See Karen Farsoun, "State Capitalism in Algeria", *MERIP Reports, No. 35, p. 17.*

19 *Karen Pfeifer, Agrarian Reform and the Development of Capitalist Agriculture in Algeria*, PH. D. dissertation, American University, Washington, D.C. 1981.

20   J. P. Durand, "Le Redressement de l'Agriculture", *Le Monde Diplomatique*, Nov. 1986, p. 36.
21   *El Moudjahid*, 30 May 1988.
22   For a comprehensive analysis of this theory see William D. Graf, "The Theory of the Non-Capitalist Road", in Brigitte H. Schulz and William W. Hansen, eds., *The Soviet Bloc and the Third World: The Political Economy of East-South Relations*, Boulder, CO: Westview Press, 1988.
23   *Middle East Executive Reports*, March 1982, p. 5.
24   *Euromoney*, October 1977, p. 64.
25   On Boumedienne's preferrence for dealing with American firms over European ones, see *Nouvelles Économiques*, 152, Feb. 1975. With regard to Algerian-US relations see William Quandt, "Can we do Business with Radical Nationalists?—Algeria: Yes", *Foreign Policy*, Vol. 7, Summer 1972.
26   *Middle East Executive Reports*, July 1983, p. 10.
27   T. Baumgartner and T. Burns, "Technology and the Development Debate: Limitations of NIEO Strategy", *Alternatives*, VII, 1981, p. 317.
28   For a discussion of Eastern Europe's export of 'turnkey' plants to the third world see Patrick Gutman, "The Export of Complete Plants with Buy-Back Agreements: A Substitute for Direct Investments in East-South Relations (a Working Hypothesis)", in Schulz and Hansen, *op. cit.*
29   *Annual Report*, Algerian Ministry of Finance, 1980.
30   J. Perrin, *Les Transferts de Technologie*, Paris: Le Découverte, 1983, p. 58.
31   See *National Charter*, Ministry of Information, 1981, pp. 82-84.
32   *Ibid.*, p. 84.
33   *Ibid.*, p. 83.
34   This is obviously applicable to the "statist" regime of Eastern Europe: *inter alia*, Khrushchev/Stalin; Brezhnev/Khrushchev; Gorbachev/Brezhnev; Honecker/Ulbricht; Gierek/Gomulka; Kania/Bierek; Dubcek/Novotny; Husak/Dubcek; etc.
35   James Scott, *Comparative Political Corruption*, Englewood Cliffs, NJ, 1972, p. IX.
36   *CNES Document*, 1971, p. 60.
37   R. Osterkamp, "L'Algérie entre le plan et le marche: Points de vue récents sur la politique économique de l'Algérie", *Canadian Journal of African Studies*, Vol. 16, No. 1, 1982.
38   *The New York Times*, May 1982.
39   James Petras, "The Peripheral State", *Journal of Contemporary Asia*, Vol. 4, 1982, pp. 418-19.
40   Said Chikhi, *Institution Syndicale et Formation Sociale*, MA Thesis, University of Algiers, March 1977, p. 50.
41   A 1980 *Report of the Ministry of Planning* (p. 23) acknowledged that at least 1.1 million young people were neither in a job nor a training program.
42   J. Schnetzler, "Les effets pervers du sous-emploi à travers l'example Algérien", *Canadian Journal of African Studies*, Vol. 14, 3, 1980, p. 465.
43   Ibn Mobarek, "La politique d'industrialisation et le développement de couches intellectuelles en Algérie, *Revenue d'histoire Maghrebine*, Nos. 27-28, Dec. 1982, p. 255.
44   *Le Monde Diplomatique*, Nov. 1986, p. 33.
45   *Le Monde*, 7 March 1984.
46   This outlet has been significantly reduced by France's recent decision to restrict the number of work and residence permits available to Algerians. This will only serve to deepen the problems associated with the disaffected urban youth.
47   The *UGTA Charter* (1969) notes (p. 128) that in the early post-revolutionary period the state was forced by militant workers by nationalize some settler-owned factories.
48   *Révolution et Travail*, 25 July 1967.
49   *Ibid.*, 20 Nov. 1967.
50   Cited in F. Weiss, *Doctrine et action syndicale en Algérie*, CUJAS, Paris 1970, p. 347.
51   *Révolution et Travail*, 23 May 1969.
52   *El Moudjahid*, 10 May 1969.

53 *Project of Labor Charter*, MTAS, p. 41.

54 *Charte et Code de la Gestion Socialiste des Entreprises*, p. 10.

55 *General Statut de Travailleur*, Article 182.

56 Dersa, *L'Algérie en débat. Luttes et développement*, Cedetim/Maspero, Paris, 1981, p. 137.

57 Said Chikhi, "La classe ouvrière aujourd'hui en Algérie", *Les Temps Modernes*, No. 432-433, 1982, pp. 57-80.

58 Although most of these have not been officially reported as such in the Algerian media, their occurance has become known through word of mouth and an inferential reading of the press.

59 Maxime Rodinson, *Marxism and the Muslim World*, New York: Monthly Review Press, 1981.

60 Since independence Algeria's population has grown from around 11 million to over 23 million by 1987. It is projected to reach 33.5 million by the year 2000. Estimates are that nearly 60 percent of Algeria's total population is under the age of 21. *World Resources 1987*, New York: Basic Books, 1987, p. 248.

61 This assertion is based upon personal observations and discussions with many of these marginalized and unemployed youth.

62 *Révolution Africaine*, No. 1256, 25 March 1988, p. 20.

63 Essay contained in *The Wretched of the Earth*, Harmondsworth: Penguin Press, 1967, pp. 119-165.

64 *Ibid.*, p. 146.

65 *Ibid.*, p. 132.

CONTRIBUTORS

Ibrahim Mohammad Al-Awaji received his Master's Degree in Public Administration from the University of Pittsburgh and his Ph.D. from the University of of Virginia (1971). He is currently Deputy Minister of the Interior Kingdom of Saudi Arabia and has to his credit several publications in English and Arabic on Arab local administration and Saudi public administration and its impact on development.

Abdelrahman Al-Hegelan obtained his Ph.D. in Political Science and Public Administration from Florida State University in 1985. He currently holds a high position in the Ministry of Finance, Kingdom of Saudi Arabia. His research interests focus on public administration and bureaucracy in the Arab World.

Nazih AYUBI teaches at the Department of Politics, University of Exeter, in Great Britain. A graduate of Cairo University, he obtained his Doctorate from Oxford University, England. He taught at Cairo University from 1975 to 1979, and was Visiting Associate Professor of Political science at the University of California, Los Angeles, from 1979 to 1983. In addition to the publication of scholarly articles in major international journals, he is the author of several books in Arabic as well as the author of *Bureaucracy and Politics in Contemporary Egypt* (London, 1980), and a contributory author to: *Rich and Poor States in the Middle East*, eds. Kerr and Yassin (Boulder, 1982); *The Iran-Iraq War*, eds. Tahir-Kheli and Ayubi (New York, 1983); *The Middle East in the 1980s*, ed. P. Stoddard (Washington, 1983); *The Arabian Peninsula*, ed. R. Stookey (Stanford, 1984); *The Mediterranean Region*, ed. G. Luciani (London, 1984); and *Beyond Coercion: Durability of the Arab State* eds. Zartmen and Dawisha (London, 1988).

Muhammad Bushara received his Ph.D. in Political Science and Public Administration from Florida State University in 1985. He is currently with the National Training Directorate, Council of Ministers, Khartoum, Sudan.

William W. Hansen received his first degree from the University of Maryland in Political Science. He received a M.A. in African Studies from the University of London, School of Oriental and African Studies and is working on a doctoral dissertation on the relationship between Black America and South Africa at Boston University. He has published articles on African Politics in several journals, including *Africa Today*, and *The Journal of Modern African Studies*. He is co-editor with Brigitte H. Schulz of *The Soviet-Bloc and the Third World: The Political Economy of East-South Relations*, to be published by Westview Press in early 1989. He presently teaches Political Science at the University of Maryland, European Extension.

Raymond A. Hinnebusch is Associate Professor of Political Science at the College of St. Catherine, St. Paul, MN, and a specialist on Egypt and Syria, political parties, peasant politics, and rural development. In addition to many articles on politics in Syria, Egypt and Libya, he has authored *Egyptian Politics Under Sadat: The Post-Populist Development of an Authoritarian-Modernizing State* (Cambridge University Press, 1985) and *Peasant and Bureaucracy in Syria: The Political Economy of Rural Development* (Westview, 1989).

Tawfic E. Farah received his Ph.D. in Political Science from the University of Nebraska (1975). He is currently President of MERG Analytica and Editor of the *Journal of Arab Affairs*. His books include: *Political Behavior in Arab States: Political Socialization in Arab States* (with Yasumasa Kuroda); and *Pan Arabism and Arab Nationalism*. He has also contributed a score of scholarly articles on the Middle East which appeared, among others, in Comparative Politics, Journal of Social Psychology, and International Journal of Middle East Studies. He has also made contributions, on a regular basis, to the Los Angeles Times and International Herald Tribune.

Joseph G. Jabbra received his Licence in Law from St. Joseph, Beirut (1965) and his Ph.D. in Political Science from the Catholic University of America, Washington, D.C. (1971). He is Professor of Political Science and Vice-President (Academic and Research), Saint Mary's University, Halifax, Nova Scotia, Canada. He has published several books and monographs and over twenty articles and book chapters, and presented over thirty papers, all dealing with the Middle East, and Canada. His latest books include *Voyageur To A Rocky Story, The Lebanese and Syrians of Nova Scotia*, co-authored with his wife, Dr. Nancy W. Jabbra and published by the Institute of Public Affairs, Dalhousie University, 1984; *People of the Maritimes: Lebanese*, also co-authored with his wife and published by East Publications, Nova Scotia, 1987; *Public Service Accountability: A Comparative Perspective*, Co-editor with Dr. O. P. Dwivedi, Kumarian Press, West Hartford, Connecticut, U.S.A., 1988. He has been the recipient of several research grants from the Social Sciences and Humanities Research Council of Canada and the Office of the Secretary of State of Canada. He is active in the International Association of Schools and Institute of Administration. His current research interests include the impact of religious fundamentalism on the formation of domestic public policy in the Middle East and law and development in the Arab world.

Jamil Elias Jreisat, Ph.D. (1968), University of Pittsburgh, is a professor of public administration and former chairman of the Department of Political Science at the University of South Florida. He has authored numerous monographs, articles, chapters in books, and a reference book (annotated bibliography). His research has been published in *Public Administration Review, Souther Review of Public Administration*, former *Journal of Comparative Administration, public productivity review*, and *Public Administration and Development*. Among his most recent publications are: *Administration and Development in the Arab World: Annotated Bibliography* (New York: Garland Publishing Inc., 1986); "Administrative Reform in Developing Countries: A Comparative Perspective", *Public Administration and Development* (Jan. 1988); and "Productivity Measurement: Trial and Error in St. Petersburg" in *Public Productivity Review* (Winter, 1987).

Ali Leila holds a Ph.D. from the University of Cairo. He has written extensively in Arabic on public policy and political development in the Arab World. He is currently Professor of Sociology at Ein Shams University, Cairo, Egypt.

Mukhtar Al Assam holds a B.A. (Honours) in Political Science (1970) and a Diploma in Public Administration (1968) from the University of Khartoum, a Master's of Social Science, Local Government and Administration from the University of Birmingham (1973), and a Ph.D. in Public Administration from the University of Wales (1977). His political career in Sudan included being, among others, Deputy Minister, Local and Regional Government and Advisor to the President (1981-1982), and Member of Parliament with Senior Minister Status (1983-1984). He taught political science and public administration at the University of Khartoum (1977-1981) and the Sudan Military Academy (1984-1985) and since 1985, he has been teaching public administration at the University of the United Arab Emirates. He has an impressive number of publications including *The Ecology of Public Administration in the United Arab Emirates* (Alain, 1988), *Local Government Reforms: The Experience of Egypt and Sudan* (Oman, 1987), and *Administrative Reform and the Arab World* (Oman, 1986).

Monte Palmer received his M.A. (1962) and Ph.D. (1964) in Political Science from the University of Wisconsin. His publications include *The Egypian Bureaucracy* (1988), co-authored with El-Sayeed Yassin and Ali Leila and published by Syracuse University Press, and *The Dilemmas of Political Development*, fourth edition, Peacock, 1989. He has also published a score of articles in refereed journals on bureaucracy and development in the Middle East. His main research areas include public administration and political development in the Middle East.

Rachid Tlemcani was educated in Algerian schools and received his first degree from the University of Algiers in Political Science. He received his M.A. and Ph.D. from Boston University. His doctoral dissertation, *State and Revolution in Algeria*, was published by Westview Press in the United States and by ZED Press in Britain. He is currently doing research on the Intifadah uprising in the West Bank and Gaza while continuing his ongoing research into the political economy of modern Africa. He is presently an Associate Professor at the Institute of Political Science at the University of Algiers where he is head of the Middle East Study Group.

El-Sayeed Yassin was educated in France and is currently Director, Al Ahram Centre for Strategic and Political Studies, Cairo, Egypt. He has published extensively in Arabic on the Middle East and he is the co-author of Rich Nations and Poor Nations (1984).

INDEX